PAST Simple

Learning English through History

DAVID RONDER AND
PETER THOMPSON

Garnet
EDUCATION

Published by
Garnet Publishing Ltd.
8 Southern Court
South Street
Reading RG1 4QS, UK

www.garneteducation.com

First published 2012.
ISBN 978 1 85964 529 1

British Cataloguing-in-Publication Data
A catalogue record for this book is available from the British Library.

Production

Project management:	Rod Webb, Nicky Platt
Editorial team:	Rod Webb, Sue Coll, Nicky Platt
Design and Layout:	Neil Collier, Mike Hinks, Bob House
Illustration:	Doug Nash
Photography:	gettyimages.com, clipart.com, corbis.com, istock.com, Mary Evans Picture Library

The authors and publisher would like to thank the following for permission to reproduce copyright material:

Extract from *Annus Mirabilis* by Philip Larkin reproduced by permission of Faber & Faber Ltd.

Every effort has been made to trace copyright holders and we apologize in advance for any unintentional omission. We will be happy to insert the appropriate acknowledgements in any subsequent editions.

Printed and bound
in Lebanon by International Press: interpress@int-press.com

CONTENTS

Introduction

'Life is one-tenth here and now,
nine-tenths a history lesson.'

Graham Swift (English novelist)

This book is based on the idea that learning about a country's history is a wonderful way to learn its language. English was born in Britain, and has both shaped and reflected British history over many centuries. History and language are intimately bound together. You cannot truly understand one without knowing something about the other.

History is traditionally narrated in the past simple tense of our title, but its richness and variety mean that all sorts of other language and structures are used, too: idioms and conditionals, for example, as well as the full range of perfect and continuous tenses. All of these (and more) appear and are explored in the book.

Past Simple consists of 22 chapters on selected aspects of British history, 12 of them on key episodes or periods such as the Elizabethan Age or First World War, the other 10 on some of the big themes (imperialism, the growth of democracy) that run through the story of these islands. Each chapter is based around a central reading text, which is followed by comprehension and critical thinking exercises, additional primary source material and a focus on relevant language points. Plenty of opportunity is also given for skills work – speaking and writing as well as reading – and there are follow-up research tasks to be done on the Internet and in libraries.

Within this regular structure, the texts themselves are presented in different ways – as conventional factual accounts, as magazine-type articles, and in the style of webpages – to ensure a varied diet for the learner.

Our aim has been to create a book on British history for learners of English, and not in any sense a definitive History of Britain. We have included the material that we consider most interesting and useful for learners of English to know, keeping the needs of would-be British citizens in mind. The book can be dipped into at will – and the **timeline** should help anyone doing so to keep their bearings – but the largely chronological arrangement means that learners can acquire an overall sense of the development of British history by starting at the beginning and working through to the end. That way they will also cover most of the main English language areas studied at intermediate level and above.

People learn best when they are engaged by the subject matter. *Past Simple* delivers English through the culturally vital medium of British history, which offers so much stimulating material that the hard part for us was choosing what to leave out. In our view, history's great advantage as a language-learning topic is that it is just so much more interesting than the typical subject matter you find in most English language textbooks. Our message to anyone using this book is: enjoy and learn.

David Ronder, Peter Thompson

Timeline of key events in British history

This timeline is selective, focusing on the key events and reigns covered in *Past Simple*. We suggest you build on it and create your own, more extensive timeline of British history.

55 & 54 BC	Julius Caesar leads expeditions of Roman soldiers into Britain from Gaul (France)
AD 43	Emperor Claudius leads a full Roman invasion of Britain
410	The Romans abandon Britain
1066	The Battle of Hastings
1215	The signing of the Magna Carta
1509-47	The reign of King Henry VIII
1558-1603	The reign of Queen Elizabeth I
1564	The birth of William Shakespeare
1588	The Spanish Armada
1642-48	The English Civil War
1649	The execution of King Charles I
1665-66	The Great Plague
1666	The Great Fire of London
1707	The Act of Union between England and Scotland
1757	Britain takes political control of India through the East India Company
1800	The Act of Union between Britain and Ireland
1807	The abolition of the slave trade in the British Empire
1832	The Great Reform Act
1837-1901	The reign of Queen Victoria
1886	The first Irish Home Rule Bill
1903	The foundation of the Women's Social and Political Union
1916	The Battle of the Somme
1927	The establishment of the British Broadcasting Corporation
1940-41	The Battle of Britain and the Blitz
1947	India gains independence from Britain
1948	The foundation of the National Health Service
1952	The start of the reign of Queen Elizabeth II
1973	Britain joins the European Economic Community
1979	Margaret Thatcher becomes Britain's first female Prime Minister
2003	America and Britain invade Iraq

1 CIVILIZING THE BARBARIANS: THE ROMANS IN BRITAIN

Section 1: *Reading*

A Before you read – think and discuss

The Roman Conquest was the first major invasion of the British Isles. Britain at that time was not a unified country. It was populated by a collection of tribes known as the Celts.

- Who were the original inhabitants of your country?
- Does your country today have any connection with its ancient inhabitants?
- Did the Romans ever rule your country?
- What, if anything, do you know about the Romans and the Celts in ancient Britain?

B Read the text

WHAT THE ROMANS DID FOR US

'From the year 400 to the year 1900, no one had central heating and very few had hot baths.' ***Winston Churchill***

In 1980, the National Theatre in London staged a play that caused outrage for its violent and explicit scenes. Although it was called *The Romans in Britain*, it told only part of the story. A truly historical play would feature much more in the way of dull practical achievement; there would be graphic road-building scenes, shockingly good engineering, and all the drama of flushing toilets.

Julius Caesar made the first official contacts between Rome and Britain in 55–54 BC, but the full Roman Conquest came nearly a century later. The Emperor Claudius decided to invade in AD 43 because he was the new Emperor of Rome and needed to prove he was a strong ruler. In order to be sure of defeating the Celts, Claudius landed with 50,000 men at the site of modern-day Richborough in Kent. The Roman occupation of 'Britannia' (most of modern-day England and Wales) was to last from AD 43–410.

Although the occupation of Britain lasted nearly 400 years, it remained incomplete. The more developed south-east was conquered quickly, though there were later **rebellions**. This success was due to diplomacy as well as arms. The Romans benefited from alliances with sympathetic native rulers, who then enjoyed favoured status. The advancing Roman army built fortresses, camps and roads and helped with construction in towns such as Camulodunum (Colchester), Britannia's first capital. The earliest towns, dating from the mid-1st century, reveal wooden houses and shops as well as stone public buildings such as temples and administrative headquarters. The Romans also brought their particular style of architecture to the countryside in the form of villas, the most impressive of which contained garden-courtyards, mosaics, wall paintings and Mediterranean statues.

Many of the native tribes in Britannia – including the Iceni, the Brigantes and the Atrebates – were initially given semi-independence by the Romans. In AD 60, the king of the Iceni died, and the Romans decided to remove this independence. They seized property and raped his daughters. The girls' mother, the tall, flame-haired Queen Boudicca, rose up in fury against the Romans. The Iceni destroyed the towns of Camulodunum, Verulanium (St Albans) and the flourishing port of Londinium (London). The Romans eventually defeated the rebels in a battle during which, according to one Roman report, 80,000 Britons and just 400 Romans were killed, though it is difficult to judge the accuracy of this report. After the battle, Boudicca was determined not to be captured. She gave her daughters deadly poison before taking her own life. According to popular legend, she is buried under Platform 9 of Kings Cross. To this day, Boudicca remains a symbol of revolt against occupation.

After the Boudiccan revolt, the Romans began to expand their area of control. The Roman province now included Wales, northern England and, briefly, southern Scotland. In AD 122, the Emperor Hadrian visited Britain. He ordered the construction of a 117 km-long stone wall from the River Tyne to the Solway Firth. Hadrian's Wall separated the Roman province from the **barbarian** north, and was a visual demonstration of the power of Rome. However, its true historical significance is that it symbolizes the failure of the Romans to conquer the whole of Britain.

The Romans brought many architectural **splendours** to Britain and also a money economy. The Roman troops had cash wages and were able to purchase items with them. The Romans started charging taxes and creating markets for their goods. Consequently, by the late 1st/early 2nd centuries AD people commonly used coins, even on the humble farms where most of the native population lived.

Cultural life in Roman Britain was complex yet harmonious. Romans and incomers from other provinces introduced their own religious customs, such as the worship of the fertility goddess Isis and the god of wine Bacchus, without destroying **indigenous** Celtic beliefs. Britons adopted romanized names, e.g., Tiberius Claudius Cogidubnus, and the elite spoke and wrote the Roman language, Latin. (Ironically, Latin still

had no word for 'grey', even after the Romans had suffered 400 years of British weather.) People also continued to speak the native language of Britannia. It survives today in Wales and Cornwall as Brythonic.

The end of Roman Britain followed a series of Empire-wide crises. Barbarians began to attack Roman provinces with greater frequency, and in AD 401–02 Rome began to withdraw troops from Britain to defend Italy. In AD 408–09, Britain was attacked by Saxons (the ancestors of the modern-day English), and in AD 410 the Emperor Honorious told the cities of Britain to 'look to your own defences'. Consequently, Roman Britain came to an end because the Romans lacked the resources, rather than the will.

A British comedian once famously asked, 'What have the Romans ever done for us?' The truth is that they brought many benefits to Britain; whether the native inhabitants of Britain *wanted* them is another question.

Glossary

rebellion	an attempt to remove a leader/government by force
barbarian	a person who did not belong to one of the major civilizations of Greece, Rome or Christianity and was therefore thought to be uncivilized
splendours	magnificent features
indigenous	native, belonging to a region

C Check your facts!

1 The first paragraph suggests that the Roman occupation of Britain was marked by:
a) violence.
b) dull practical achievement.
c) both of these.

2 Which Roman Emperor played a greater role in the conquest of Britain: Julius Caesar or Claudius?

3 'The Romans destroyed many things in Britain, and created nothing.' True or false?

4 Boudicca was the leader of the:
a) Brigantes.
b) Albions.
c) Iceni.
d) Artebrates.

5 Why did Hadrian build a wall in the north of Britain?

6 How did the Romans change the British economy?
a) They began paying people wages.
b) They cut taxes for the poor.
c) The majority of people started using money.
d) Only common people used coins.

7 'The Romans imposed Catholicism on the British.' True or false?

8 'The Romans could have stayed in Britain but they didn't want to.' True or false?

9 What does the writer think the Romans did for us?
a) nothing
b) everything
c) impossible to say
d) quite a lot

D What do you think?

1 According to the second paragraph, is it fair to say that Emperor Claudius was:
a) inexperienced?
b) stable?
c) just about to retire?
d) none of the above?

2 Boudicca was 'flame-haired'. This means she was:
a) red-haired.
b) yellow-haired.
c) hot-tempered.
d) a woman with highlights in her hair.

3 Boudicca poisoned her daughters because:
a) they fought against her.
b) she didn't want them to see her take her own life.
c) they had exaggerated the number of dead Britons.
d) she did not want the Romans to capture them.

4 Why do you think the author finds it remarkable that even after 400 years in Britain, the Romans had no word for 'grey'?
a) The Romans had over 30 words for rain.
b) Their uniforms were red, black and grey.
c) Great engineers usually love the colour grey.
d) The sky in Britain, unlike the Mediterranean, is often grey.

5 Explain what you understand by the phrase 'look to your own defences'.

Section 2: *Topic development*

A Roman architectural splendours

amphitheatre	baths	fortress	lighthouse	mosaic	viaduct

1

2

3

4

5

6

Label pictures 1–6 with words from the box. Use a dictionary if necessary.

B The linguistic context

1 Even though the Romans left Britain in AD 410, Latin-origin words have continued to enter the English language ever since. Below are some common Latin terms in English. Match these words to their meanings. Use a dictionary if necessary.

a) et cetera (etc.)	**1** brief account of a person's life/career
b) abacus	**2** dictionary grouping words with a similar meaning
c) thesaurus	**3** study programme/course
d) post-mortem	**4** and so on
e) curriculum	**5** counting machine
f) CV (curriculum vitae)	**6** investigation into cause of death

2 The words also tell us something about British history. Use their meanings to help you fill in the table below by matching each term to when it first appeared in English. One has been done for you as an example.

period	historical background	Latin term
1100s–1400s	Legal business and bureaucracy grew considerably, with lists and inventories becoming more common.	
1500s	Trade and the money economy expanded.	
1600s	English dictionaries and grammars began to be written.	*thesaurus*
1700s	Medicine began to become more scientific.	
1800s	Education expanded rapidly and became more organized.	
1900s	Recruitment and applying for jobs became more professional.	

C The Warrior Queen

This statue of Boudicca stands by Westminster Bridge in London, near the Houses of Parliament. Study the statue and discuss the following questions.

1 How would you describe the statue? What image do you think it is trying to project?

2 It was commissioned during Queen Victoria's time, when interest in Boudicca grew enormously. Why do you think this was?

3 How do you think it makes British MPs feel as they pass it on their way to work?

4 Do you like it? Why/why not?

D And finally ...

A survey found that British people regarded the words in the speech bubble, spoken by the character of Julius Caesar in a comedy film about the Romans, to be the best one-line joke ever in movie history.

> *'Infamy! Infamy! They've all got it in for me!'*

Do you understand the joke? If not, try saying the words aloud with a partner. Can you hear the play on words?

If you need to use a dictionary, look up *infamy* and *to have it in for someone*.

Section 3: *Extension activities*

A Discuss

The Romans considered themselves to be civilized and dismissed everything non-Roman as barbarian/uncivilized.

- Why do you think the Romans saw things in this way?
- What is your idea of civilization?
- How would you measure a country's civilization – its technology, education, culture, attitudes, friendliness, etc.?
- Do you think Britain is a civilized country? Give reasons.

B Research

Search for: 'Hadrian's Wall' 'Picts' 'Ninth Legion of Rome' 'All roads lead to Rome' 'Rome wasn't built in a day' 'When in Rome, do as the Romans do'

1 Use the Internet and/or a library to answer the following questions:
  - **a)** How much of Hadrian's Wall is still standing?
  - **b)** How long would it take you to walk from one end to the other?
  - **c)** Who were the Picts and what do we know about them?
  - **d)** What happened to the Ninth Legion of Rome?
  - **e)** Find the titles of a book and a film connected with this story.

2 Go on YouTube or similar to watch the famous scene from Monty Python's *Life of Brian* where the rebels discuss the question 'What did the Romans ever do for us?'. Make a list of all the things that are mentioned. What kind of film is this? Is the Monty Python group British or American?

3 Discuss with a partner what the following expressions about Rome mean, then use the Internet or a library to find out when they first entered the English language.
  - 'All roads lead to Rome.'
  - 'Rome wasn't built in a day.'
  - 'When in Rome, do as the Romans do.'

Do you use the same expressions in your language?

C Write

Write a short essay discussing the statement below. Include arguments for and against, and say whether you agree or not. (250 words)

'It is better for a country to have good roads, public order, central heating and hot baths than to be free.'

TIP!

Try to give examples from your own country's history or from what you know about British history.

2 1066 and all that: The Norman Conquest

Section 1: *Reading*

A Before you read – think and discuss

The last time that England was successfully invaded was in 1066. Other countries have been invaded and occupied much more recently and much more often.

- Why has England not been invaded for such a long time?
- Has your country been invaded in the last 1,000 years?
- How does the experience of invasion and occupation affect the people living through it?
- What reasons are there for invasions?

B Read the text

File Edit View Favorites Tools Help

1066 and all that: The Norman Conquest

'Then began the death-bearing clouds of arrows. There followed the thunder of blows …'
Henry of Huntingdon, *Historia Anglorum*, c. 1130

Fact file

- 5th January 1066: King Harold II **succeeds** Edward the Confessor, who had no sons, as King of England
- Sunday 14th October 1066 – Battle of Hastings
- Harold killed during the battle – thought to be by an arrow in his eye
- 25th December 1066 – William crowned King of England
- December 1085 – Domesday Book commissioned by William as a land survey of the whole of England
- 9th September 1087 – William dies

The last invasion of England

The Battle of Hastings was the decisive victory in the Norman conquest of England. On Saturday 14th October 1066, the Normans of Duke William of Normandy (later known as William the Conqueror) defeated the Saxon army led by King Harold II, only eight months after Harold had succeeded to the English throne. Many people think that famous date marks the beginning of English history, as it was the last time the country was conquered by a foreign power. Comparing the significance of the event to that of the Bolshevik revolution, a Russian diplomat once said to an English diplomat: 'You had your 1917 in 1066.'

William – heir to the English throne?

William believed that he was the heir to the English throne and claimed that Harold had **sworn an oath** accepting this. William travelled with the blessing of the Pope, who did not recognize Harold as king and had given William a ring and a banner to show that God was on his side. He crossed the Channel from

France in boats that his soldiers had made with their own hands. When they arrived on the Sussex coast there was no one to resist the invading force. But as William walked up the beach, he tripped and fell on his face in front of his troops. Turning this embarrassment to a show of confidence, he rose with his hands full of sand and shouted, 'I now take hold of the land of England!' Everyone cheered.

The battle

William arrived unopposed because Harold's army was distracted by the Viking invasion of the north of England. After defeating the Vikings in Yorkshire, they had to march 250 miles south in only twelve days. Not surprisingly, they were exhausted by the time they reached the south coast. To make matters worse, the Battle of Hastings lasted all day, which was unusual at this time when most battles were over within an hour.

The two armies had between 7,000 and 8,000 men each, but William's army included **cavalry**. A lack of **archers** made the English hesitant. Late in the battle, a mixture of genuine and mock retreats by William's army drew the English forces down from their defensive position on the ridge – where the town of Battle now stands. Then, according to the Bayeux Tapestry, King Harold was hit in the eye by an arrow before falling to the ground. It is believed that he was finished off by a Norman horseman, some say by William himself. The Normans then poured through the English ranks and **routed** them.

The Norman victory at Hastings was decisive, despite approximately 2,000 Normans being killed and wounded in the battle. Saxon casualties, including Harold's two brothers, were greater still. But more importantly, Edgar the Atheling, the only surviving male member of Edward the Confessor's family, failed in his attempts to organize further resistance.

The Bayeux Tapestry

While some facts are known, most of what actually happened in the battle is unclear. There are, however, some records that we can use. The most famous is the Bayeux Tapestry, which is both an artistic masterpiece and a crucial historical source. The belief that Harold was hit in the eye with an arrow stems from a famous scene in the tapestry which shows a Saxon noble being wounded in this way. This huge visual narrative was the work of Norman women, possibly for the Conqueror's half-brother Odo, who can be seen in the tapestry playing an important role in the battle.

William crowned

Two months later, on Christmas Day 1066, William was crowned King of England in Westminster Abbey. Three years after that, he had imposed his rule over most of England and Wales. He built huge, **impregnable** stone castles like the Tower of London and then terrorized the inhabitants of the surrounding countryside into obedience.

Domesday Book

William wanted to raise taxes from the inhabitants of his new kingdom and did not want anyone to avoid paying them. He knew that knowledge is power, so he sent his men to conduct the first doorstep survey in history. They went to every village in England and wrote down exactly who owned what and how much. The findings were written up in a huge book known as the Domesday Book (1086). According to the Treasurer of England, it was given this name because 'it is not permissible to contradict its decisions, any more than it will be those of the Last Judgement' (*dome* or *doom* was the old English word for judgement). Remarkably, the Domesday Book was used to settle a dispute as recently as 1982.

New English aristocracy

The ruling class of England, and much of the rest of Britain, was recreated by the Norman Conquest. Many current-day British aristocrats can trace their ancestry back to the Conqueror's men; the words *noble*, *gentle* and *aristocrat* themselves come from the French.

Death of William

William died after a riding accident in September 1087. Some reports from that time suggest that on his death-bed he was seized by guilt at the way he had taken the crown from Harold. Three of his sons survived him, but he refused to appoint an heir: 'Having made my way to the throne of that kingdom by so many crimes, I dare not leave it to anyone but God alone.'

C Check your facts!

1 Who won the Battle of Hastings?
2 Who supported William in his conquest of England?
3 Why was Harold's army tired?
4 William's army had something that Harold's lacked completely; Harold's army also needed more of something else. Name both.
5 How many of William's men were killed in the battle?
6 Give two reasons for the importance of the Bayeux Tapestry.
7 How did William impose his rule over England?
8 How did the Normans get detailed information about the English?
9 What are the ruling class called in England?
10 How long did William rule England?

D What do you think?

1 Whose side was the Pope on in 1066? Why?

2 After his fall on the beach, William rose with his hands full of sand because:
a) it represented England itself.
b) England would be like sand running through his fingers.
c) it was an important natural resource.
d) he had never seen sand before.

3 Who tried to organize English resistance?
a) Alfred the Great
b) Harold's brothers
c) Edgar the Atheling
d) King Lear

4 'William waited until he had imposed his rule on the greater part of England before having himself crowned.' True or false?

5 What is the Domesday Book?
a) a list of who owned what and how much
b) the laws of Old England
c) names of doorstep tax-payers
d) predictions about the Last Judgement

Glossary

succeeds	takes over from (as king)
sworn an oath	spoken a promise before God
cavalry	soldiers on horses
archers	soldiers with bows and arrows
routed	completely defeated
impregnable	cannot be taken

Section 2: *Topic development*

A Dictionary task

The cartoon opposite is perhaps a typical example of British humour in the way it makes light of a serious matter. Use a dictionary to find out the meaning of the **idiom** used – *one in the eye.*

1 Now see if you can match these eye idioms to their meanings without using the dictionary:

to see eye to eye	to watch over
to catch the eye	to ignore something bad or wrong
to turn a blind eye to	to agree with
to keep an eye on	to hide the truth from someone
not to bat an eyelid	to attract attention
to pull the wool over someone's eyes	to show no sign of stress or emotion

2 Check your answers in the dictionary, then try to put the idioms in the sentences below, using the correct form.

a) Someone has to stay at home and ____________________ the children.
b) My boss and I ____________________ on all the important issues.
c) He ____________________ when I told him the terrible news, he just sat there looking calmly at me.
d) Well, dressing like that does rather ____________________, I can't help looking at him.
e) Somehow she got away with it; I think they decided to ____________________ to her wrongdoings.
f) Everyone cheated in the class tests, the teacher was young and inexperienced and it was easy to ____________________.

3 Find three things that you and your partner see eye to eye about.

B The Bayeux Tapestry

The picture below shows Norman women stitching the Bayeux Tapestry. Completed in 1082, the tapestry depicts in a uniquely vivid way the Norman invasion of England in some 70 scenes, with brief explanatory 'captions'. It is about 70 metres long and half a metre wide.

1 Study the pictures a–c on page 16, showing sections of the tapestry, and match the caption below to the right one:

Normans set fire to an English house

2 Now write simple captions for the other two pictures.

a

b

c

C How the Normans complicated English spelling

Study the brief text below and then complete the task that follows.

After the Norman Conquest, French scribes introduced several new spelling conventions. A number of Old English forms were replaced, such as *qu* for *cw* (*quick*). The scribes replaced *h* by *gh* in such words as *might* and *enough*, *c* by *ch* in *church*, and *u* by *ou* in *house*. They began to use *c* before *e* and *i* in such words as *city* and *cell*. Because the letter *u* was written in a very similar way to *v, i, n*, and *m*, they tried to ease the reading task in some sequences of those letters by replacing *u* with *o* (*come, love, one, son*). By the beginning of the 15th century, English spelling was a mixture of the two systems – Old English and French.
– Crystal, David. 2nd edition (2003). *The Cambridge Encyclopedia of the English Language*, Cambridge University Press.

1 Write the following words in their Old English spellings:

quick ***enough*** ***church*** ***house*** ***city*** ***love***

2 Which spellings do you think are easier to remember, old or new? Why?

D The Norman invasion of vocabulary

The Normans brought thousands of Latin and French words into English, which until then had been a largely Germanic language. For obvious reasons, these new words tended to be related to law and administration, but also to medicine, art, fashion and food. Sometimes they replaced existing Old English words, but in most cases they existed alongside them, though they had a more formal meaning.

Put the following French-derived words for types of meat into the correct box to match their Old English equivalent, using a dictionary if necessary.

venison pork mutton veal beef

Old English	French-derived
ox	
pig	
sheep	
calf	
deer	

Section 3: *Extension activities*

A Discuss

We have seen how the Normans began the process of complicating English spelling. As you know by now, English spelling can be difficult for anyone learning the language, because words don't always look like they sound or sound like they look.

- Some people say we should change the rules and simplify English spelling. Do you think this would be a good idea?
- Would it be easy? Can you think of any problems?
- Do you know of any other examples of countries that have tried to simplify their spelling? What happened?

B Research

Search for: 'historical re-enactment' + 'Battle of Hastings' / 'William the Conqueror' + 'route to London' / 'Domesday Book' + 'legal dispute' + '1982'

Use the Internet and/or a library to answer the following questions.

a) Who re-enacts historical battles, and particularly the Battle of Hastings? Are the re-enactments realistic? What do you think motivates people to do this?

b) Trace the route William and his troops took to London after the Battle of Hastings. Did they face any serious resistance along the way?

c) Find out more about the legal dispute that was settled using the Domesday Book in 1982. Why did it need to be used? Could it still be used to settle disputes in English law?

C Write

1066 is one of the most famous dates in English history. Write about a famous date in the history of your country, saying why it is important and whether you think it is remembered in the right way. (250 words)

3 Majesty and marriages: King Henry VIII

Section 1: *Reading*

A Before you read – think and discuss

When Henry VIII was young, the people idolized him; as he got older, they became terrified of him.

- Has your country ever been ruled by a tyrant?
- Do tyrants achieve some good things, or only bad things?
- What is the character of a tyrant like? Is it very different from an ordinary person's character?
- What, if anything, do you know about Henry VIII?

B Read the text

MAJESTY AND MARRIAGES:
HENRY VIII AND THE REFORMATION

'A fool, a liar and a damnable rotten worm.' *Martin Luther on Henry VIII*

Henry VIII was arguably the most brilliant, but certainly the most powerful and terrible of all English monarchs. Henry's court was spectacular and he was the first monarch to be addressed as *Majesty*. He was also a great patron of the arts. But no king has been so **ruthless** with those who challenged him. Paranoid and cruel, he was both a hero and a monster.

Henry was a strikingly handsome and charming 17-year-old when he became King of England in 1509. He was particularly admired for his physical **prowess** – he was an expert horseman, wrestler, archer and dancer. He was also fluent in French, Spanish and Latin, and was an accomplished musician. The famous scholar Erasmus proclaimed that Henry was 'a universal genius'.

The young king seemed to have everything. He personally led three successful military campaigns in France on horseback. In 1521, the Pope granted him the title 'Defender of the Faith' after Henry had written an attack on Martin Luther (leader of the Protestant Reformation, Europe's revolution against the Catholic Church). But after nearly 20 years of marriage to Catherine of Aragon (the widow of his elder brother, Arthur), Henry still lacked the one thing he wanted more than anything else – a son. He had become convinced that a series of failed pregnancies and stillbirths were the result of God's displeasure. The evidence was in the Bible: 'If a man shall take his brother's wife, it is an unclean thing … they shall be childless.' All Henry needed was the Pope's permission to divorce Catherine. He had a ready-made replacement in Anne Boleyn, a self-assured beauty ten years his junior who was already pregnant with his child.

The Pope's refusal to grant Henry a divorce **unleashed** forces whose consequences are still felt today. In 1534, Henry formally broke with the Roman Catholic Church and granted himself a divorce from Catherine. He then proclaimed himself head of the Church of England. This was the English Reformation and it gave Henry sweeping new powers which he was quick to use. He destroyed 600 monasteries and sold their land.

Anne Boleyn's marriage to such a man was to prove fatal for her. Her 'crime', like Catherine's before her, was her failure to produce a son. Henry wanted the marriage to end and so bent the truth for his own purposes. Thus, Anne's naturally flirtatious nature was used as definitive 'proof' of **adultery**. Men were tortured and absurd 'confessions' were produced. A court musician pleaded guilty to adultery. Anne's own brother was charged with having sex with her.

On the morning of Anne's execution (19th May 1536), she said: 'I hear the executioner is very good, and I have a little neck.' By that time, Henry was already on his way up the Thames to see Jane Seymour. The couple were engaged the very next day and married ten days after that. Jane was able to give Henry what he desperately wanted, a male heir. It was, however, a difficult birth and Jane died from a fever less than two weeks after giving birth. Her death brought Henry great sorrow. It was later said that her name was on Henry's lips when he died in 1547, and he was buried next to her.

Henry was to marry three more times: to Anne of Cleves in 1540; to Catherine Howard, who was executed for adultery in 1542 along with her lover and three other members of the royal household; and finally, in 1543, to Catherine Parr, who survived him. Henry's ever-changing private life was matched by his increasingly extreme public policies. He behaved with great cruelty not only to those who he believed had betrayed him but also to those who were closest to him. This included his brilliant ministers Thomas Cromwell and Cardinal Thomas Wolsey. The former was executed on 28th July 1540; the latter died while facing charges of high treason. One historian has written: 'His most enduring conviction was that next to God, he knew best.'

A ruined monastery

The final years of Henry's reign, which Charles Dickens called 'a spot of blood and grease upon the history of England', saw a descent into **tyranny.** Both Henry's appearance and conduct were transformed. Between the ages of 23 and 45 his waist measurement increased gradually from 89 cm to 114 cm. By 1541, his waist measured 137 cm, his chest 145 cm. He became too obese to walk, so a small cart was built to transport him around the royal palace at Hampton Court. His enormous size led to a variety of physical ailments. He had foul-smelling breath, his legs were covered in leaking boils and fungus, and he suffered from chronic **haemorrhoids**. Research suggests that his violent mood swings may have owed something to the complete lack of vitamins in his diet. Henry would touch neither vegetables nor fruit – he simply ate vast amounts of meat and drank immense quantities of alcohol.

In his 36-year reign, Henry **squandered** his many advantages. He came to the throne rich but left huge debts and a currency which had lost its value. As a result of his father's 'divorcements and such mischiefs', the sickly boy king Edward VI was given an impossible legacy. Henry's rule had been arbitrary, cruel and driven by anger. And as the Duke of Norfolk warned, 'The consequence of royal anger is death.'

Glossary

ruthless	hard and cruel
prowess	skill, ability
unleashed	released
adultery	having sex with someone other than your marriage partner
tyranny	cruel and oppressive rule
haemorrhoids	swollen veins in the bottom
squandered	wasted

C Check your facts!

1 'Henry VIII was a cruel monster because he lacked culture.' True or false?

2 'The young Henry was good at sports but not very bright.' True or false?

3 Who was the father of Anne Boleyn's baby?
a) Martin Luther
b) Henry VIII
c) Henry's brother, Arthur

4 When did England officially cease to be a Catholic country?

5 What was the real reason Henry had Anne Boleyn executed?
a) She tortured men.
b) She failed to produce a son.
c) She was unfaithful to him.
d) She was too friendly with the Pope.

6 Which two things make Jane Seymour different from Henry's other wives?

7 Who else was executed with Catherine Howard?

8 'Between the ages of 23 and 45, Henry's waist grew by more than 1 cm a year.' True or false?

9 How long was Henry the King of England?

D What do you think?

1 Henry is described in the text as paranoid. This means:
a) he had breathing difficulties.
b) he couldn't walk and had to be pushed around in a cart.
c) he was suspicious and mistrustful of others.
d) he was a deeply religious man.

2 Do you think Henry believed in God? Find reasons to support your answer in the text.

3 Henry 'ate vast amounts of meat' and 'drank immense quantities of alcohol'. This means:
a) he drank more than he ate.
b) he ate more than he drank.
c) he ate and drank quite a lot.
d) he ate and drank an awful lot.

4 'Charles Dickens believed that Henry VIII was one of England's greatest kings.' True or false?

5 The text talks of Anne Boleyn's 'crime', the 'proof' of her adultery and the 'confessions' produced. These words are in inverted commas to show:
a) that they were spoken by someone at the time.
b) that the author does not believe that what is being said is true.
c) how they were written in Henry VIII's time.
d) that they are more important than the other words in the paragraph.

Section 2: *Topic development*

A Henry's six wives

Look at the timeline below of Henry VIII's reign and marriages. Then answer questions 1–4.

1509	Henry crowned King of England
1509-33	married to Catherine of Aragon
1533-36	married to Anne Boleyn
1536-37	married to Jane Seymour
Jan-July 1540	married to Anne of Cleves
July 1540-42	married to Catherine Howard
1543	marries Catherine Parr, who survives Henry
1547	Henry dies

Hans Holbein

Portrait of Henry VIII by Hans Holbein

1 'Henry outlived all his wives.' True or false?

2 Which wife was Henry married to for longest?

3 Which was the shortest marriage?

4 What is the longest period that Henry went without a wife?

B Judging by appearances

When Henry was looking for a fourth wife, he sent the artist Hans Holbein to paint a portrait of Anne of Cleves. Henry was charmed by the flattering portrait and decided to marry her. However, when Henry actually met Anne, he was appalled by how ugly she was. He supposedly compared her to a horse, and the marriage was soon over.

1 Look at the portraits 1–6. Discuss which one you think is Anne of Cleves.

1

2

3

4

5

6

2 Write descriptions of the six women. Describe their appearance and what you think their personalities were like. Use the words in the boxes to help you. (An example has been done for you below.)

Appearance: eyes nose chin complexion hair neck figure headdress ring necklace fair/dark thin/fat tall/short

Personality: shy friendly happy/sad strong/weak fun/serious

Example:

She is wearing a black dress and a necklace with a 'B' on it. She has dark hair and eyes. Her figure is slim. She seems friendly and fun.

3 Read your description to your partner. Can he/she guess which portrait you have described?

4 Do you think it is possible to judge someone's personality from his/her appearance? Discuss your ideas.

Section 3: *Extension activities*

A Discuss

- Henry VIII was a mighty king but a very bad husband.
- Do you think it is possible to be a leader and have a happy private life?
- Do you think we are more interested in the private lives of leaders today than in the time of Henry VIII?
- When judging leaders, should we pay any attention to their private lives?

B Research

> **Search for:** 'Greensleeves' 'Fantasia on Greensleeves'
> 'Henry VIII' + 'ailments' + 'remedies'
> 'Hampton Court Palace' 'Queen of England ' + 'nine days'

1 Search the Internet to read the lyrics and listen to the tune of *Greensleeves*.
   a) Investigate the relationship between the song and Henry's relationship with Anne Boleyn.
   b) Investigate claims that Henry wrote the words. Do you think he wrote them? Why/why not?

2 Find out which famous 20th-century English classical composer wrote *Fantasia on Greensleeves*.

3 Research some of the strange remedies Henry VIII used to try to cure his ailments. Did any of them work?

4 Go to the official website of Hampton Court Palace. Why do so many people get lost there?

5 Six years after the death of Henry VIII, there was a Queen of England who reigned for just nine days. Use the Internet to find out about her. What was her title? Why was her reign so short?

C Write

Just before Anne had her head cut off, she said to the crowd, 'I pray God save the king and send him long to reign over you, for a gentler nor a more merciful prince was there never: and to me he was ever a good, a gentle and sovereign lord.' Write an alternative speech for her, telling the truth about Henry VIII. (200 words)

4 Good Queen Bess: Elizabeth I

Section 1: *Reading*

A Before you read – think and discuss

Elizabeth I was one of England's greatest queens, who won a famous victory against the powerful Spanish Armada.

- What great battles have there been in your country's history?
- Has a woman ever led your country in a time of war?
- What, if anything, do you know about Elizabethan England?

B Read the text

GOOD QUEEN BESS: ELIZABETH I

'I know I have the body of a weak and feeble woman, but I have the heart and stomach of a king, and a king of England too.'

Queen Elizabeth I to her troops at Tilbury, before the arrival of the Spanish Armada

Fact file

- 7th September 1533: birth of Elizabeth
- 1547: father Henry VIII dies
- 1554: Elizabeth is imprisoned in the Tower of London
- 17th November 1558: Elizabeth becomes Queen of England
- 1587: Mary Queen of Scots, Elizabeth's cousin, is executed for plotting against her
- July 1588: Spanish Armada is defeated
- 24th March 1603: Elizabeth dies

Birth of a daughter

There was just one problem with the birth of the child who would later become Queen Elizabeth I – she was supposed to be a boy. The pre-written court letters announcing the birth had to be quickly changed. The word *prince* became *princes* (the Elizabethan spelling of *princess*) with the addition of a letter 's'. This unwelcome surprise would cost the child's mother, Anne Boleyn, her life (see Chapter 3). It nearly proved fatal for Elizabeth herself.

Threats to the young Elizabeth

Elizabeth was the daughter of a **demonized** mother, so it is remarkable that she managed to survive the reign of Henry VIII. When Henry died, Elizabeth was in even more danger. Her Protestant half-brother became King Edward VI and declared that she was **illegitimate**, with no right to be queen. After his death, Elizabeth's Catholic half-sister became Queen Mary I. Queen Mary imprisoned Elizabeth in the Tower of London, and tried to collect evidence to show that Elizabeth was plotting against her.

Elizabeth becomes Queen

Not only did Elizabeth survive these threats but she became queen herself when Mary died. Mary had no heir, so Elizabeth became the third of Henry's children to sit on the throne in 11 years. Elizabeth remained queen for 45 years, and became the most idolized of all British monarchs. Today, she is still celebrated as one of England's finest monarchs, who successfully fought off England's enemies while ruling over a period of extraordinary cultural flowering.

Her father's daughter?

Elizabeth was very like her father in many ways. She looked like Henry, with her father's hair and skin colour, nose and lips. She had much of Henry's character, too – his intelligence, his strong personality, his eloquence and his irresistible **charisma**. But unlike her father, she believed in mercy and she was prepared to compromise. She was a practical ruler who avoided extremes – in religion, in politics and (usually) in punishment.

To marry or not

One of the first challenges for the attractive young queen was the question of marriage. Throughout her reign she had a succession of male favourites, most notably Robert Dudley, Earl of Leicester, but she never married. She explained this by saying, 'I am already bound unto a husband, which is the kingdom of England.' It seems Elizabeth realized that marrying a foreign prince would threaten England with foreign domination, while marrying an English nobleman could cause trouble at home.

The Virgin Queen

Elizabeth's powerful image was as Gloriana the Virgin Queen – a golden-haired, white-faced icon in jewels and spectacular dresses. She was not afraid to use her power – from 1563, portraits of Elizabeth had to be copied from an approved template. When a preacher criticized the Queen in 1579 because she did not want to marry, she ordered that his writing hand should be chopped off. 'God save the Queen!' he cried out after his right hand was severed, raising his hat with his left hand.

The Church of England

Elizabeth followed a cautious path in matters of religion. She restored the Church of England's independence from Rome and under her leadership blended both Protestant and Catholic elements, although it remained technically Protestant. She expected people to conform outwardly and to respect her position as head of the church. However, she was not concerned about their inner beliefs. 'I would not open windows into men's souls,' she explained.

Execution of Mary Queen of Scots

Some Catholics believed that Elizabeth's Catholic cousin, Mary Queen of Scots, should be Queen of England. Mary had been **ousted** from the throne of Scotland and fled to England, where she was put under **house arrest**. Mary became the focus of numerous Catholic plots against

Elizabeth's life. There were many years of conspiracies concerning Mary and warnings about the threat she represented. Eventually, Elizabeth could take no more and Mary was tried and executed.

The Spanish Armada

By now, religious tensions across Western Europe were extremely high. The Catholic Philip II of Spain was outraged by the execution of Mary, and by English attacks on Spanish ships and possessions in the New World. He decided to send a massive **Armada** against England. The plan was that a fleet of 130 ships would sail from Spain to the Spanish Netherlands. Here, they would pick up a Spanish army and sail for England. However, the Armada was seen in the Channel and **beacon** fires were lit across England. The English navy, under the command of Sir Francis Drake, prepared itself. In Tilbury, Kent, the Queen addressed her troops. She gave one of the most inspiring speeches in English history (see quote on previous page). The English navy, helped by the weather, divided and conquered the Armada, to the eternal glory of Elizabeth.

Elizabeth's legacy

Elizabeth ruled England with tremendous style, spirit and flair. She symbolizes the defiant, patriotic liberty of the English perhaps better than any other national figure. During the time of her reign, it was believed that it was against God's will for a woman to hold power. Her triumph in a man's world is, therefore, all the more remarkable.

Glossary

demonized	described as evil
illegitimate	child born of parents not lawfully married to each other
charisma	charm, star quality
ousted	removed (from a position of power)
house arrest	imprisonment in your own home
Armada	(historical) armed Spanish fleet
beacon	warning/signal

C Check your facts!

1 'Anne Boleyn died giving birth to Elizabeth I.' True or false?

2 Which one of these was not Henry VIII's child?
a) Elizabeth
b) Robert
c) Mary
d) Edward

3 Is Elizabeth considered the finest monarch to rule Britain?

4 'Elizabeth's personality was just like that of her father.' True or false?

5 What danger was there in Elizabeth marrying a) a foreigner and b) an Englishman?

6 When the preacher who lost his hand asked God to save the Queen, he meant:
a) Elizabeth.
b) the Virgin Queen.
c) Gloriana.
d) all of the above, because they are the same person.

7 'Elizabeth was more tolerant of different religious beliefs than her father.' True or false?

8 In what way did Mary Queen of Scots pose a threat to Elizabeth?

9 Where was the Spanish army that should have invaded England?
a) Spain
b) on the Armada
c) Tilbury
d) the Spanish Netherlands

10 In what way could you say Elizabeth was a modern woman?

D What do you think?

1 What does the added 's' in the pre-written court letters tell us more about: English spelling or attitudes towards women in Elizabeth's day? Explain your answer.

2 The text says that Elizabeth 'avoided extremes – in religion, in politics and (usually) in punishment'. Why do you think the word *usually* is inserted before *punishment*? Is there anything in the text that helps to explain this?

3 Write your own interpretation of Elizabeth's phrase, 'I would not open windows into men's souls'.

4 Explain what the expressions below mean. Use the context to help you.
patriotic liberty
cultural flowering
approved template

5 What do you feel is the most remarkable thing about Elizabeth? Give reasons for your choice.

Mary Queen of Scots

Section 2: *Topic development*

A The very image of a queen

Elizabeth I was short (about 163 cm) and her teeth were black with decay. Yet the royal portrait painters never showed this. Instead they showed an idealized image of Elizabeth, the mighty Virgin Queen married to England. Pictures of her were full of symbolic meaning, a style that was typical of the period.

Study the picture, painted not long after Elizabeth's victory over the Armada. Identify items a)–e).

a) the defeated Armada
b) the triumphant British fleet
c) a symbol of Elizabeth's purity (clue: she is wearing these)
d) a symbol for the New World
e) a symbol of Elizabeth's imperial rule

B A mysterious object

1 Read the passage below about a legend relating to Sir Francis Drake. He is one of the heroes of the Elizabethan age, famous for being the first Englishman to sail round the world.

What is the missing four-letter word that goes in every blank?

2 Discuss in pairs or small groups:
- Do you think there is any truth in the legend?
- Are there similar legends in your country's history? Explain them.
- Whether true or not, do you think countries need such legends? Give your reasons.

Drake's __________ is a __________ that Sir Francis Drake took with him when he sailed round the world. Shortly before he died, he ordered the __________ to be taken to Buckland Abbey, where it still is today, and vowed that if England was ever in danger someone was to beat the __________ and he would return to defend the country. According to legend it can be heard to beat at times when England is at war or a significant national event takes place.

Several times throughout history, people have claimed to have heard the __________ beating, including: when the *Mayflower* left Plymouth for America in 1620, when Admiral Lord Nelson was made a freeman of Plymouth, when Napoleon was brought into Plymouth Harbour as a prisoner, and when World War I began in 1914.

Reportedly, on HMS *Royal Oak*, a victory __________roll was heard when the German navy surrendered in 1918. The ship was then searched twice by the officers and then again by the captain and neither a __________ nor a __________mer were found on board and eventually the phenomenon was put down to the legendary __________.

In 1938, when Buckland Abbey was partly destroyed by fire, the __________ was rescued and taken to safety. Plymouth was devastated in the air raids that followed, reminding some of the ancient legend that "If Drake's __________ should be moved from its rightful home, the city will fall." The __________ was returned and the city remained safe for the rest of the war.

Section 3: *Extension activities*

A Discuss

Queen Elizabeth effectively said that she was married to her job when she described England as her husband.

- Do you think leaders must sacrifice their personal lives to do their jobs properly?
- How does this affect their performance in the job – does it make them less 'human'?
- What would it be like to be married to a great leader?
- Is it possible to have a normal life if you are a great leader or are married to one?

B Research

Search for: 'Hatfield House' 'Walter Raleigh' + 'cape' + 'tobacco' 'execution of Mary Queen of Scots'

1. Elizabeth I was brought up at Hatfield House. Use the Internet to find out as much as you can about this place. Where is it? Can you visit? What would you see if you went there?
2. Use the Internet to find out about Sir Walter Raleigh. What stories are there about him, connected to Elizabeth? How and when did he die?
3. Find and read an account of the execution of Mary Queen of Scots. Who did she forgive at the time of her death?

C Write

Watch a film about Elizabeth I (there are many of these). Then write a review. Include details about:

- the story.
- the characters.
- the performance of the actress playing Elizabeth – is it convincing?
- whether it helps you understand what life was like during that time.
- whether you would recommend it, and why.
  (250 words)

5 Roundheads and Cavaliers: The English Civil War

Section 1: *Reading*

A Before you read – think and discuss

The English Civil War was a series of armed conflicts fought between Parliamentarians and Royalists which played a key role in the development of parliamentary democracy.

- What major battles have there been in your country?
- Why/how were the battles won?
- Who were the leading figures involved on either side?
- What, if anything, do you know about the English Civil War?

B Read the text

Roundheads and Cavaliers:
The English Civil War

'Whose blood stains the walls of our towns and defiles our land? Is it not all English?'

Bulstrode Whitelocke, 17th-century lawyer, writer and parliamentarian

Isaac Foot, a well-known British intellectual, once said that he judged any man he met by his answer to a question about events 300 years earlier. The question was, 'On whose side would you have fought in the Battle of Marston Moor?' He was referring to the largest battle of the English Civil War, which took place just outside York on 2nd July 1644. On one side were the 'Cavaliers', the army of the Stuart King, Charles I, and on the other the 'Roundheads', the army of the English Parliament.

The Civil War (1642–48) was a series of such battles but also a conflict in people's hearts and minds. It climaxed with the execution of the King and the creation of the only republic the country has ever had. The clash between King and Parliament revolved around the most fundamental question – how should the country be ruled? Differences in religion and politics bitterly divided families and split friend from friend. Modern estimates suggest that one in every four or five adult males was caught up in the fighting. Around 150 towns were destroyed, 11,000 houses were burnt or demolished and 55,000 people were made homeless. Nearly 4 per cent of England's population, roughly 100,000 people, died in the fighting or from war-related disease.

The causes of the Civil War were complex but can be reduced to a few simple factors. Charles I was a weak, indecisive yet extraordinarily stubborn character who believed utterly in the divine right of kings. This meant he believed his power came from God and that no mortal soul was allowed to question his authority. Charles refused to allow Parliament to sit from 1629 to 1640 (a period known as the 'Eleven Years' Tyranny'), but Parliament was full of lawyers and historians who were no longer prepared to accept royal **absolutism**.

By 1642, a series of arguments over religion, finance and the limits of parliamentary power led both the King and Parliamentarians to recruit men from all over the country who were prepared to choose a side to fight on. On 22nd August, outside the city of Nottingham, Charles raised his personal flag. This was his formal declaration of war. But the **omens** were not good: that night, Charles's flag and most of his temporary headquarters were blown down in a ferocious storm.

October 1642 saw the first great battle of the Civil War at Edgehill, north of Oxford. The outcome was inconclusive. The following year, the balance of power swung the King's way. But in July 1644 the two sides met at Marston Moor and the Parliamentarians were triumphant. After the battle the plain-spoken commander of the parliamentary cavalry, Oliver Cromwell, boasted that 'God made them as **stubble** to our swords'. This gentleman farmer was becoming the inspirational figure of the parliamentary cause. Cromwell was a deeply committed **Puritan** with a revolutionary approach to recruiting men. He was uninterested in their social background and simply wanted 'plain, honest men' who had 'the root of the matter in them'.

The Puritan religion was the inspiration behind the New Model Army, a 22,000-strong professional fighting force that Cromwell and the parliamentary commander Sir Thomas Fairfax created in the spring of 1645. Its regiments sang **hymns**, did not swear or drink alcohol, and were guided by **sermons**. Royalists mocked the New Model Army soldiers for supposedly bending their heads constantly in prayer. But the sober discipline and religious certainty brought dramatic results. On 14th June 1645, at Naseby in the East Midlands, Cromwell's red-uniformed men won the decisive battle of the Civil War, taking some 5,000 prisoners and securing £100,000 (£11.2 million today) in jewels and money. Worst of all,

Statue of Oliver Cromwell

from Charles's point of view, the Roundheads also captured private letters from the King which revealed he was plotting to hire foreign soldiers and to repeal the laws against Roman Catholics. For Cromwell and his fellow Puritans, this was the ultimate betrayal. It was proof that the King could not be trusted.

Charles surrendered to a Scottish army in 1646 but his endless plotting restarted the conflict in 1648. The outcome was the same as before, but this time the personal consequences were fatal. The King was now denounced as 'Charles Stuart, that man of blood', and a small number of the most extreme parliamentarians, led by Cromwell, forced an act through Parliament which allowed Charles to be tried for **treason**. Although the trial took place in the open, its outcome was clear from the start. On a bitterly cold morning in late January 1649, Charles was publicly beheaded. With the words 'behold the head of a traitor', the executioner lifted Charles's severed head from the floor and displayed it to the horrified crowd. Many were convinced that this was such an extraordinary act that God Himself would immediately split the skies open and bring an end to the world. This did not happen of course, but Charles remains the only English monarch to have been executed.

Glossary

absolutism	power without limits
omens	signs
stubble	what's left in the fields after crops have been cut
Puritan	extreme Protestant, believing that the Bible is the literal word of God and that man's destiny is fixed
hymns	religious songs
sermons	religious lectures
treason	betrayal of the country

C Check your facts!

1 Where was Marston Moor?

2 What were the two major results of the Civil War?

3 'The majority of English people fought in the Civil War.' True or false?

4 Choose the adjective which does **not** describe King Charles I.
a) weak
b) simple
c) stubborn
d) indecisive

5 Who started the Civil War, the King or Parliament?

6 'The outcome of the battle at Edgehill was inconclusive.' This means:
a) Parliament won.
b) the King won.
c) no one won.
d) we don't know who won.

7 Why was the capture of the King's private letters so significant?

8 How many English kings have had their heads chopped off?

D What do you think?

1 Which of the following was **not** a factor in the outbreak of the Civil War?
a) religion
b) the power of Parliament
c) money
d) head-bobbing

2 The question about which side to fight on at Marston Moor is designed to find out:
a) how democratic someone is.
b) how good a fighter someone is.
c) how religious someone is.
d) how English someone is.

3 Explain your understanding of 'plain, honest men' who have 'the root of the matter in them'.

4 Which of the following believed God was on their side in the Civil War?
a) Both Charles I and Oliver Cromwell.
b) Neither Charles I nor Oliver Cromwell.
c) Only Oliver Cromwell.
d) Only Charles I.

5 'Charles was actually more revolutionary than Cromwell because he refused to let Parliament sit and acted as an absolute ruler.' Do you agree with this statement? Explain your answer.

Section 2: *Topic development*

A When Did You Last See Your Father?

1 What do you think is happening in the painting? Discuss your ideas.

This famous picture, painted in the 19th century by W. F. Yeames, shows a Royalist family who have been captured by the enemy. We can tell from the boy's clothes that he is a Royalist, and from the title of the painting that he is being questioned about where his father is.

2 Which of the following best describes the boy's attitude? Discuss your ideas.
   - a) frightened and confused
   - b) proud and brave
   - c) jokey and relaxed
   - d) he thinks it's all a big game

3 Read the descriptions below and find the people in the painting.
   - a) This man is leaning forward with his chin resting on his hands and seems almost sympathetic towards the boy.
   - b) This man is a clerk, writing down everything that is said. His presence makes the scene seem more official and like a court case.
   - c) This girl is dressed in Royalist clothing so we can assume that she is the boy's sister. She is crying, probably because she is afraid of what the soldiers might do to her family. It may also be her turn next to be questioned.

4 Find two more people in the painting and write descriptions of them. Read them to your partner. Can he/she find the people?

B Name this child

The deeply religious nature of the Puritans was reflected in the names they gave their children. Here are some examples:

Be-thankful | Fear-the-Lord | Fight-the-good-fight-of-faith | From-above

Hate-evil | Jesus-Christ-came-into-the-world-to-save | Make-peace

Love-well | Praise-God | Sorry-for-sin | What-God-will

1 Do people give their children religious names today? Think of some examples.

2 What words characterize your classmates? Brainstorm some alternative names for each other. Then discuss whether you would give your child a 'unique' name like this.

C Wrong but Wromantic versus Right and Repulsive

W. C. Sellar and R. J. Yeatman were two English schoolteachers. In the 1930s, they wrote a brief history of England called *1066 and All That*. This humorous book was a light-hearted reworking of the history of England, and the authors came up with some alternative accounts of the key events in English history. Writing on the Civil War, they stated that it was a struggle between the Cavaliers, who were 'Wrong but Wromantic', and the Roundheads, who were 'Right and Repulsive'. Read their account of the outbreak of the Civil War below.

> Charles I was a Cavalier King and therefore had a small pointed beard, long flowing curls, a large, flat, flowing hat, and *gay attire*. The Roundheads, on the other hand, were clean-shaven and wore tall, conical hats, white ties, and *sombre garments*. Under these circumstances a Civil War was inevitable.

1 Which picture is of Charles I and which of a Puritan?

2 Was fashion really the cause of the Civil War? Why do you think the authors suggest that it was?

3 Why do you think Sellar and Yeatman spelt *Wromantic* with a silent *w*? How many other English words, apart from *wrong*, can you think of with a silent *w*?

4 'Gay attire' meant:

a) clothing with a provocative style.
b) frills round the neck.
c) feathers in your hat.
d) cheerful and colourful clothes.

5 Choose the word which best describes *1066 and All That*.

a) scholarly
b) humorous
c) Cavalier
d) sombre

6 Discuss whether it is better to be Wrong but Wromantic or Right and Repulsive.

Section 3: *Extension activities*

A Discuss

Oliver Cromwell believed that God was guiding him in the Civil War. A biography of him by historian Christopher Hill is titled *God's Englishman*.

- What do you think the title means?
- What happens when political leaders believe God is on their side? Can you think of any modern examples?
- What might be the dangers of mixing politics and religion?
- Is there a place for religion in politics?

B Research

Search for: 'English Civil War Society' + 'Bill Bailey re-enactment'   'warts and all' + 'Cromwell'   'Cromwell' + 'Christmas'   'Humpty Dumpty' + 'Civil War'

1 Search for 'Bill Bailey re-enactment' and watch a video of a British comedian making fun of people like members of the English Civil War Society. Discuss whether you think there is any truth in this view of them.

2 The expression *warts and all* came from the instruction Oliver Cromwell gave to the artist painting his portrait: 'Mr Lely, I desire you would use all your skill to paint my picture truly like me, and not flatter me at all; but remark all these roughnesses, pimples, warts and everything as you see me, otherwise I will never pay a farthing for it.' Use a dictionary or search the Internet to find out what *warts and all* means. Then write three sentences using the phrase.

3 Search using the words 'Cromwell' and 'Christmas' to find out what happened to Britain's biggest festival under the Puritans. Discuss what would be a suitable Christmas present for a Puritan.

4 Search the Internet to discover the connection between the traditional children's nursery rhyme 'Humpty Dumpty' and the Civil War.

C Write

'On whose side would you have fought in the Battle of Marston Moor?' Answer this question, giving your reasons. (250 words)

6 FIRE AND PLAGUE: Samuel Pepys' London

Section 1: *Reading*

A Before you read – think and discuss

Samuel Pepys is one of the most famous writers in the English language, even though he never intended his work for publication. His *Diary* tells of two of the most terrible disasters in the history of London.

- What sort of things do people put in their diary?
- Do people write differently if they think no one will read it?
- Why do you suppose Samuel Pepys' *Diary* is so famous?
- Pepys lived through the Great Plague and the Great Fire of London. What effect do you think this had on his writing?

B Read the text

File Edit View Favorites Tools Help

Samuel Pepys

'Both the most ordinary and the most extraordinary writer you will ever meet.'

Claire Tomalin (journalist and biographer whose biography of Samuel Pepys won the Whitbread Award in 2002)

The importance of Samuel Pepys

Students of **Restoration England** have a unique advantage over students of other periods of British history. These students can step into the bustling life of everyday London through the magic doorway of Samuel Pepys' *Diary*. Pepys kept his *Diary* in shorthand and completed it in secrecy. It was eventually published in 1825 and was an instant success. Pepys has remained a **household name** to this day.

A colourful decade

The decade that Pepys **chronicled** in his *Diary* was remarkably colourful. Above all, he is most famous for his vivid descriptions of day-to-day life during the Great Plague of 1665–66 and his record of the Great Fire of London of 1666. This was perfect material for his curiosity and powers of observation. His writing is fresh and direct. While other diarists focused on

Fact file

- 23rd February 1633: Samuel Pepys born in London.
- One of 11 children.
- January 1660–May 1669: Pepys writes his diary.
- 1665–66: Pepys lives through the Great Plague, when about 100,000 people died.
- September 1666: Pepys also experiences the Great Fire of London that starts in a baker's shop in Pudding Lane and lasts for three days.
- 1703: Pepys dies aged 70 but has lived long enough to see a new London emerge from the ashes of 1666, including Sir Christopher Wren's magnificent St Paul's Cathedral.
- Pepys once said, 'My mind is with child to see any strange thing.' Perhaps this is why he continues to exert such power.
- Schoolchildren learn that a typical diary entry opens with 'Up betimes' and closes 'And so to bed'.

politics or spiritual affairs, Pepys' interests were more human. His *Diary* reflects his fascination with the way people behave: their greed, ambitions, jealousies and scandals.

A personal account

Pepys never intended to publish his diary and because of this he reveals the most embarrassing details of his life – being set upon by a small dog, being spotted with a mistress, being terrified by a pillow and falling into a ditch. He always speaks his mind: the food at a friend's house 'stunk like the devil'; Shakespeare's *A Midsummer Night's Dream* is 'the most … ridiculous play I ever saw in my life'. He also presents a truthful picture of himself, including his cruel treatment of his long-suffering wife Elizabeth. He even describes an agonizing operation to remove a bladder stone, which he **characteristically** kept in a special case to show off to friends.

Humble origins

Pepys' father was a tailor; his mother had been a domestic servant. From these humble origins, Pepys rose rapidly in the world. He was, in his own words, 'a very rising man'. This owed a great deal to some helpful connections. It was a time of great naval expansion, and his cousin Sir Edward Montagu got him a job in the Navy Office. He started as Clerk of the King's Ships and ended up running the **Admiralty**. Unusually for the era, he worked hard and opposed corruption. He was also an MP and President of the Royal Society, as well as a man about town and a figure in royal circles.

Living through the plague

Pepys was living and working in London when the plague began in May 1665. The disease spread with frightening speed in the narrow, smelly streets and rat-infested slums of London. In the summer heat, thousands of people died every month, and all who could afford to fled from the city. But Pepys stayed and observed what was happening with appalled fascination. Houses where the plague had struck were closed up and a red cross painted on the door with the inscription 'Lord have mercy on us'. At night, carts rumbled through the deserted streets, gathering up the dead and dumping them into pits for common burial. One of Pepys' diary entries in late August 1665 begins on this haunting note: 'But now, how few people I see, and those walking like people that have taken leave of the world.'

The Great Fire of London

Life in the City was just about returning to normal when the Great Fire broke out. Pepys described the 'poor people staying in their houses … till the very fire touched them.' As darkness fell, he saw the fire spread 'in corners and upon steeples, and between churches and houses … in a most horrid, malicious, bloody flame.' This resulted in the dreadful noise of 'the cracking of houses at their ruin.' King Charles II personally supervised the blowing up of buildings to make a fire break. Little could be done, however, until the wind dropped and the fire burned itself out. By that time the old City of London had been destroyed, and the great church of St Paul was a hollow shell.

The final years

Pepys stopped writing his diary only three years after the Great Fire because he feared he was losing his eyesight. He did so with a heavy heart. It was, he wrote, 'almost as much to see myself into my grave.' But his eyes recovered and his professional career flourished. Pepys said that the era of the reign of Charles II (1660–85) began with 'a clap of laughter', and when we read his *Diary* we can see what he meant. It reveals him as a charmingly honest though **deeply flawed** man. Reading his diary today is like having an energetic and amusing companion who brings a distant and sometimes grim age to life.

Glossary

Restoration England	England in the reign of Charles II, after Cromwell's death
household name	a very well-known person (or thing)
chronicled	recorded, told the story
characteristically	in a way that is typical
Admiralty	government department responsible for the Navy
deeply flawed	having big weaknesses, imperfect

C Check your facts!

1 How many years after Pepys started his diary was it published?

2 Which of the following would you not find in Pepys' *Diary*?
a) an account of the Great Plague
b) brilliant theatre criticism
c) embarrassing details of his life
d) an account of the Great Fire of London

3 'Pepys was very private and revealed no details of his life in his *Diary*.' True or false?

4 Pepys was never:
a) an MP.
b) an Admiral.
c) President of the Royal Society.
d) Clerk of the King's Ships.

5 What were the two main reasons for the streets being so empty during the plague?

6 'The Great Fire broke out when the plague was at its worst.' True or false?

7 Why did Pepys stop writing his diary?
a) He had lived long enough.
b) His eyesight was failing.
c) He had a heavy heart.
d) He was busy with his career.

D What do you think?

1 The 'magic doorway of Samuel Pepys' *Diary*' refers to:
a) a popular doorway in 17th-century London.
b) a secret doorway in Pepys' house.
c) an enchanted doorway.
d) a doorway of the imagination.

2 Why was British naval expansion important to Pepys' life?

3 Why do you think the London poor stayed in their houses?

4 Why did Charles II want to blow up buildings during the Great Fire?
a) To stop the fire from spreading.
b) To silence the dreadful cracking noise.
c) To give fire-fighters a break.
d) To clear the way for a new London.

5 What exactly do you think Pepys meant when he said, 'My mind is with child to see any strange thing'? Write it in your own words.

Section 2: *Topic development*

A An innocent nursery rhyme?

For generations, British children have sung a sweet song which involves them holding hands in a ring and all falling down at the end. But despite its innocent-sounding words and childish tune, many people believe 'Ring a ring of roses' is actually about the Great Plague.

1 The words of the song are in the left-hand column below. Work with a partner to match each line to one of the four beliefs about the plague in the right-hand column.

Traditional British nursery rhyme	Four beliefs about the plague
Ring a ring of roses	1 Painful sneezing was a symptom.
*A pocketful of posies**	2 A ring of red sores round the mouth was one of the first signs.
Atishoo! Atishoo!	3 Almost everyone who got it died.
We all fall down.	4 Carrying sweet-smelling flowers protected you from the plague.

*small bunches of flowers

Others argue that two of these beliefs were untrue and that the song was just childish nonsense. They point to the fact that it first appeared in print in 1881, long after the Great Plague.

2 Discuss with a partner.

a) Which two beliefs are most likely to be false?

b) Now discuss if you think the song really is about the Great Plague or is just an example of childish nonsense. Give your reasons. (Note: nobody actually knows for sure!)

B Great Fire

Below you will find an extract from Pepys' *Diary* on the day the Great Fire started. Read it carefully, then work with a partner to answer the questions that follow.

2 September 1666

Jane [Pepys' maid] called us up about three in the morning, to tell us of a great fire they saw in the City. So I rose and slipped on my nightgown, and went to her window ... but ... I thought it far enough off; and so went to bed again and to sleep. About seven [I] rose again to dress myself, and there looked out at the window, and saw the fire not so much as it was and further off. ... [Then] Jane comes and tells me that she hears that above 300 houses have been burned down to-night by the fire we saw, and that it is now burning down all Fish-street, by London Bridge.

So I made myself ready ... and walked to the Tower, and there got up upon one of the high places ... and there I did see the houses at that end of the bridge all on fire, and an infinite great fire on this and the other side the end of the bridge ... So down, with my heart full of trouble, to the Lieutenant of the Tower, who tells me that it began this morning in the King's baker's house in Pudding-lane, and that it hath burned St. Magnus's Church and most part of Fish-street already.

1 Was Pepys worried when he first saw the fire? Why/why not?

2 What do you think the word *hath* means in the second paragraph? Do you think it is a) a spelling mistake by Pepys or b) an example of the English of his time?

Section 3: *Extension activities*

A Discuss

When Samuel Pepys thought the Great Fire might burn his house down, he buried his favourite wine and Parmesan cheese in the garden. Discuss:

- what this tells us about Pepys.
- if you can sympathize with his choice of things to save from the fire.
- what you would try to save from a fire.
- how important you think material objects are when life is in danger.

B Research

Search for: http://www.pepysdiary.com/ + 'FAQs' 'Pepys' *Diary*' + 'publication' 'the Monument' + 'London'

1 Find out about the site **http://www.pepysdiary.com/** and read a full day's entry from Pepys' *Diary*.

a) How does the site choose which entry to put up each day?
b) Why do the entries change at 11 p.m. (UK time) each night?
c) What was the most interesting thing that happened in Pepys' world on the day you looked?

2 Find out about the discovery of Pepys' *Diary*.

a) Where was the code to Pepys' diaries found – where, when and how?
b) Who decoded it and how long did it take?
c) Where is it kept today?

3 Find out about the Monument in London.

a) Where exactly is it?
b) Which tube station is it nearest?
c) When and why was it built?
d) Can you visit it today?
e) What can you do there?

C Write

Keep a diary in English for a week. Write about whatever you like, but try to relate it to what has happened that day. You can be as personal and honest as you wish (like Pepys), but don't forget that your teacher is going to read it! End the entry for each day with the words 'And so to bed', as Pepys sometimes did.

7 The Longest Reign
The Victorians

Section 1: *Reading*

A Before you read – think and discuss

Britain's power was at its height during the Victorian age, when Queen Victoria reigned. However, the era is also associated with negative things like terrible factory conditions and cruel treatment of children.

- When was your country at its most powerful?
- Did everyone in the country benefit at this time?
- Who was (were) the most important leader(s)?
- What do you know about the Victorian era, if anything?

B Read the text

THE LONGEST REIGN: *The Victorian Era*

'The history of the Victorian age will never be written: we know too much about it.'

Lytton Strachey (British writer and biographer of Queen Victoria)

If the 20th century was the American century, the 19th was the British and it was a period of breathtaking change. Britain's monarch for most of that time was Queen Victoria, whose reign stretched from 1837 to 1901. Much of Britain's physical appearance today dates from the Victorian era. Millions live in houses that were built by the Victorians. Many town halls, libraries, theatres, museums, universities and churches also date from that time.

The achievements of the age were built on economic success. By the mid-19th century, Britain proudly called itself the 'workshop of the world'. It was the first fully mature industrial society, producing vast quantities of coal, iron, steel, ships and textiles. The free-trade policies of successive governments boosted Britain's dominance of world trade. Well over half of the world's goods were transported on British ships. Technological inventions seemed to shrink the world. In 1851, the first cross-Channel telegraph cable was laid from Dover to Calais. News could now travel much faster between Europe and London. In 1866, a similar cable was laid across the Atlantic, linking Britain directly to the USA.

This economic transformation of Britain was marked by major population movements from rural to industrial areas. By 1901, a remarkable 80 per cent of Britons lived in towns. They developed modern infrastructures for education, public transport, drinking water, **sewerage**, and gas and electricity supplies. Britain's banking and commercial sector became fully established, employing hundreds of thousands in offices and banks. Railways transformed not only communications but also the landscape itself. Victorian engineers built new bridges, stations and tunnels for the steam-powered locomotive engines which reached speeds of over 100 miles per hour. On the roads, the first internal combustion engines marked the start of the age of the motor car.

Yet millions were forced to make great sacrifices for these developments. The labourers (also known as *navvies*) who built the railway lines suffered a higher death rate than the British soldiers who had fought in the Napoleonic Wars against France. The celebrated author Charles Dickens exposed the extreme hardship suffered by poor working-class townsfolk in novels such as *Oliver Twist* and *Hard Times*. The Victorian **slums**, factories and workhouses remain **potent** symbols of the human cost of progress.

Politically, the Victorian age was a golden age of Parliament. More people got the vote and the party system gradually emerged. The rivalry between the Conservative and Liberal parties was **personified** by Benjamin Disraeli and William Gladstone in the 1860s and 1870s. The Conservative Party is traditionally the party of wealth and privilege. But thanks to the brilliant and witty Disraeli, it won considerable support from working-class voters. Gladstone, a deeply serious, highly principled and reform-minded man, was Liberal prime minister a record four times. He left a substantial and positive mark on the country as a whole, but he failed to win the approval of his monarch. Queen Victoria adored the flattery and attention she received from Disraeli, not least after he made her Empress of India in 1877. But she despised Gladstone. 'He always addresses me,' she once protested, 'as though I were a public meeting.'

The Victorians were very private in their social habits. Because of this, 'Victorian' can mean oppressively formal, even **prudish**. In middle- and upper-class society, manners and appearance were everything. No one ever dared mention sex. Some Victorians even dressed their piano legs in little skirts, for the sake of modesty. Their serious-minded behaviour was reflected by their monarch, who wore black for the rest of her life after the death of her beloved husband, Prince Albert, in 1861. In her declining years, she was widely associated with the phrase 'We are not amused'. She meant that *she* was not amused, but it expressed how many of her subjects felt, too.

Though it is often thought that the Victorians were too busy getting things done to have much time for fun, they did put on The Great Exhibition of 1851. Thousands of exhibits were displayed to capture the mood and values of the nation in the spectacular iron and glass Crystal Palace in Hyde Park. Most of the exhibits were British-made and the display was shamelessly self-congratulatory. It aimed to show the world just how inventive, rich and economically supreme the British were. The Exhibition coincided with a period of social peace, both in Britain and abroad. With the Victorians leading the way, the path of industry suddenly became a moral one which could ensure continued peace, progress and prosperity.

Victoria's 64-year reign finally ended in January 1901. By then, the nation was feeling far less self-confident. The Second Boer War (1899–1902) was proving surprisingly difficult to win. Britain's economic domination was also beginning to face serious challenges from its main competitors, the USA and Germany. In 1900, the Labour Party grew out of various socialist societies and trade unions. This signalled the end of the dominance of the two traditional parties. In the years up to the outbreak of the First World War in 1914, more and more Britons had reason to **mourn** the passing of the longest reign. Many of them had believed the power and superiority it symbolized would last forever.

Glossary

sewerage	drains for toilet waste
slums	very overcrowded and bad housing occupied by poor people
potent	strongest and hardest
personified	represented by a person
prudish	shocked by sexual things
mourn	be sad because something/someone no longer exists

C Check your facts!

1 'British towns now look completely different from how they did in the Victorian era.' True or false?

2 Name three important British industries in the Victorian era.

3 Population movement in Victorian Britain was mainly:
a) from the countryside to towns and cities.
b) between different towns and cities.
c) from towns and cities to the countryside.
d) between different parts of the country.

4 'It was more dangerous to work on the Victorian railways than to fight in the Napoleonic Wars.' True or false?

5 Name the two most important political parties of the Victorian age.

6 Queen Victoria wore black after 1861:
a) for the sake of modesty.
b) to show that she was not amused.
c) because her beloved husband had died.
d) to show that she was more of a private figure than a public one.

7 What was the Crystal Palace made of?

8 'Queen Victoria's reign ended on a national high.' True or false?

D What do you think?

1 Victorian Britain was the 'workshop of the world'. This meant:
a) it made most of the world's goods.
b) its workers were cheaper than those of other countries.
c) most of its people worked in shops.
d) all its people did was work and shop.

2 The percentage of the world's goods carried on British ships was about:
a) 45 per cent.
b) 50 per cent.
c) 60 per cent.
d) 85 per cent.

3 Give two reasons why Queen Victoria preferred Disraeli to Gladstone.

4 Does the word 'Victorian' have a more positive or negative meaning in modern English, according to the text?

5 The phrase 'We are not amused' revealed that Victorian Britons:
a) didn't enjoy visiting the Crystal Palace.
b) were rather serious-minded about life.
c) had no sense of humour at all.
d) were alarmed by the rise of socialism.

EXHIBITION SUPPLEMENT TO THE ILLUSTRATED LONDON NEWS
SATURDAY, JULY 19, 1851.
THE GREAT EXHIBITION.

Section 2: *Topic development*

A Queen Victoria: Fifteen facts and one lie!

1 All of these facts about Queen Victoria are true – except for one. Read the facts and discuss which one is not true. Use the phrases in the box to help you.

I'm fairly sure that … is true. It must be true. It can't be true. It might be true. What about …? Why do you think that? If X is true, Y can't be. I just don't believe it. I'm not sure about …

a She had 9 children and 40 grandchildren, and became known as the 'grandmother of Europe'.

b Her husband's father was her uncle.

c She was the first monarch to live at Buckingham Palace.

d Disraeli was her special favourite among politicians.

e She was buried with a piece of her manservant John Brown's hair, a picture of him and his mother's wedding ring on her hand.

f She loved Ireland and donated £2,000 of her own money to help in the potato famine.

g She never ate another potato after the Irish famine.

h Her mother tongue was German and she never spoke perfect English.

i A young man once tried to shoot her with a gun loaded with paper and tobacco.

j The first time she travelled in a train, she complained it was too fast at 20 mph (30 kph).

k She was made Empress of India in 1877.

l She became known as the 'Famine Queen' and was much criticized for allowing the Irish to starve.

m She wore black from Albert's death in 1861 until she died in 1901.

n She did not like black funerals. On the day of her own funeral, London was decorated in purple and white.

o She started the tradition of brides wearing white at their weddings.

p She was the first known carrier of haemophilia* in the royal family.

*when your blood does not thicken as it should, for example, when you cut yourself

2 Write ten facts about yourself, including one lie. Show them to a partner. Can he/she guess which one is the lie?

B The Queen's English

1 Queen Victoria is famous for using the Royal *We*, particularly in the expression 'We are not amused' when she meant 'I am not amused'. Choose the best explanation of why she said *we* instead of *I*:

a) She was a native German speaker and often made little mistakes in English.
b) It showed that she represented a whole nation and institution, not just herself.
c) She always thought of herself as being together with her dear husband Albert.
d) It meant that both the Queen and God were speaking together in her person.

2 Queen Elizabeth II and the modern royal family are widely thought to prefer the formal *one* to *we* when speaking about their feelings and attitudes, e.g., 'One is not amused' and 'One hopes that the weather improves'. Decide if this form is:

a) an incorrect use of the Royal *We*.
b) a variation on the Royal *We*.
c) the complete opposite of the Royal *We*.
d) the feminine form of the Royal *We*.

3 Another phrase the young Queen Elizabeth II was famous for using was 'My husband and I'. No doubt Queen Victoria used it too on many occasions. However, the Royal seal of approval does not stop people making grammatical mistakes when they use expressions like this.

In the sentences below, **b** is grammatically correct but **a** is not. Which of the other two sentences is correct, **c** or **d**?

(**Clue**: Is ***I*** the *subject* or *object* of the sentence?)

a) They have invited my husband and I to dinner.
b) My husband and I are delighted with the invitation.
c) My husband and I will arrive shortly before 8 p.m.
d) A taxi will come for my husband and I around midnight.

Can you correct the two wrong sentences? What's the rule?

Section 3: *Extension activities*

A Discuss

Victorian society appears prudish in comparison with modern British society. Discuss:

- which of the two societies' attitudes is better, in your opinion.
- which of the two is closer to your own country's attitudes.
- if you think British attitudes today are still a little Victorian.

B Research

Search for: 'Dickensian' 'Victorian bathing machine' 'Gladstone' + 'Disraeli' 'Oliver' + 'Consider Yourself' 'Scrooge'

1 Look up the word *Dickensian* in a good dictionary. Then search the Internet for 'Dickensian conditions' to find examples of the word used in modern contexts. Make notes about what you read.

2 Search the Internet to find out about the Victorian bathing machine.
   a) What was the machine's main purpose?
   b) What does this confirm about Victorian morality?
   c) When did the legal segregation* of male and female bathing areas end in Britain?
   d) What is the significance of this date in terms of Queen Victoria?

   *separation

3 Search the Internet for pictures of William Gladstone and Benjamin Disraeli. Note down the differences in their physical appearance and dress.

4 Go to YouTube and enter the search terms 'Oliver!' + 'film' + 'Consider Yourself' to enjoy a show-stopping song from a famous musical based on a Dickens novel. Which novel was the film based on? Then search for 'Scrooge' to find examples of films, cartoons and shows based on another Dickens story. What is the title of this book?

C Write

Queen Victoria wore black for 40 years. Write a short essay about wearing black. Include the following:

- who wears black in your country and why
- the meaning of black clothes in your culture
- whether you ever wear black, when and why
- how black makes you feel
- whether you think we need to change our ideas about black
  (250 words)

8 A long way from Tipperary: The First World War

Section 1: *Reading*

A Before you read – think and discuss

The First World War was one of the greatest catastrophes ever to happen to Britain. A whole generation was affected by the conflict, and Britain was never as powerful or confident again.

- Was your country involved in the First World War in any way?
- Has your country suffered from similar catastrophes? How are they remembered?
- What do you think is meant by *world* war?
- What, if anything, do you know about Britain and the First World War?

B Read the text

LIONS LED BY DONKEYS?

'The Somme is like the Holocaust. It revealed things about mankind that we cannot forget. It can never become the past.'
Pat Barker **(prize-winning English novelist)**

It is impossible to understand modern Britain without understanding its part in the First World War. The war ended at 11 a.m. on 11th November 1918; every year since then, people in Britain stop what they are doing at the eleventh hour of the eleventh day of the eleventh month, and remain silent for two minutes. On the second Sunday of each November, many British people also gather at war memorials to honour the war dead. They wear red paper **poppies** to represent the huge numbers of these flowers which grew in the disturbed soil of the battlefields. The colour of the poppies also symbolizes the blood of those who died. People still visit the war cemeteries in France and Belgium, where the graves of those who died in the Great War are lovingly looked after.

On 4th August 1914, Britain went to war against Germany in defence of Belgium, which Germany had invaded. But the real purpose of Britain entering the war was to prevent Germany dominating Europe and threatening the British Empire, with the help of its Austrian and Turkish allies. Everyone expected the war to be short and glorious: the German Kaiser told his troops that they would be home 'before the leaves fall off the trees'; in Britain, people said 'it will all be over by Christmas'. Their confidence was horribly mistaken. This long, grim war was indeed over by Christmas – but Christmas *1918*. By the time the guns finally fell silent, Britain had suffered huge casualties: 750,000 dead and 1.6 million wounded.

The vast majority of these casualties were on the Western

Front – two opposing lines of trenches stretching 760 km from Switzerland to the North Sea. It has been claimed that the huge numbers of deaths along this Front occurred because the ordinary soldiers, the 'lions', were led by 'donkeys' – incompetent generals with no understanding of the horrors suffered by soldiers trying to obey impossible orders. The tragedy was the constant repetition of the same outdated tactic: the mass charging of enemy lines, even though the enemy was now armed with modern, deadly machine guns. These tactics, used by both sides, resulted in maximum advances of just a few kilometres up until spring 1918.

The British were involved in dozens of terrible clashes, the most **notorious** being the Battle of the Somme in 1916 and the Third Battle of Ypres (Passchendaele) the following year. At both the Somme and Passchendaele, hundreds of thousands of British soldiers attacked in wave after wave supported by massive gunfire. Foot soldiers armed with rifles, bayonets and hand grenades raced across no man's land towards the enemy. But **trench warfare** gave the defending army a huge advantage. The British soldiers were met by a hail of bullets from machine guns. If an attacking soldier was lucky enough to avoid the bullets, he would have to face further, lethal obstacles – barbed wire, landmines and poison gas.

On 1st July 1916, the first day of the Somme, the British army suffered probably the worst ever day in its military history: 20,000 dead and 40,000 wounded. At that time, the army still consisted of volunteers rather than conscripted soldiers. The battle continued until November 1916, by which time mounting losses threatened Britain's ability to carry on fighting in 1917. The British attempted to use their new 'wonder weapon', the tank, but it was too slow and often broke down as rain turned the land into a sea of mud. The dead and wounded, and even sometimes the fit, **sank** into it **without trace**.

The chief strategist behind both of these battles was Field Marshal Douglas Haig. He was convinced that the Germans would run out of soldiers if he continued to attack. The Prime Minister, David Lloyd George, was utterly against

the tactics of his most senior general. His feelings are summed up in his comment that Haig was 'brilliant – to the top of his boots'. But for a variety of reasons, Lloyd George was unable to remove him and he remained in his position until the end of the war – and perhaps this was for the best. The way in which the war ended surprised Britain and its allies as much as it did the Germans. Using innovative tactics, Haig launched a counter-offensive that proved devastatingly effective. On 8th August, in what became known as the German army's 'black day', they suffered 75,000 casualties for very little loss to the British. Many German troops surrendered, realizing that no hope of victory remained. Germany's defences were smashed in just six days.

The joy of victory did not last for long, however, as people considered the huge sacrifices that had been made. By the 1920s, most people accepted that the fallen heroes of the war had been victims of a pointless struggle. And yet throughout the war, the **morale** of British soldiers remained surprisingly high. Music and laughter had helped the soldiers cope with the suffering. Their songs have been described as a 'protest of life against death'. The simple but powerful words, like those below, rose above the inhumanity of the war itself:

What's the use of worrying?
It never was worthwhile.
So, pack up your troubles in your old kit bag
And smile, smile, smile.

Glossary

poppies	red flowers that often grow wild in fields
notorious	famous for something bad
trench warfare	when soldiers fight in trenches dug opposite each other, often for long periods of time and with little progress
sank without trace	disappeared downwards, leaving nothing
morale	enthusiasm and confidence

C Check your facts!

1 Is it fair to say that the First World War still matters to modern-day Britons?

2 Who thought the war would be over sooner, the British people or the German Kaiser?

3 'Lions led by donkeys' means:
a) war made ordinary soldiers and their officers behave like beasts.
b) the ordinary soldiers were brave and the officers were foolish.
c) the ordinary soldiers were stupid and the officers were brave.
d) the British were fierce and courageous but too stubborn.

4 In trench warfare at the time of Passchendaele, was it easier to attack or defend?

5 What is the significance of 1st July 1916 for the British military?

6 Did the politicians always support the generals?

7 'General Haig was a useless general who contributed absolutely nothing towards the defeat of the Germans.' True or false? Explain your answer.

8 The attitude of most people in the 1920s towards the war was that:
a) it had been a triumph for Britain.
b) the sacrifice had been worthwhile.
c) it had wasted many lives.
d) all of the above.

D What do you think?

1 Make a list of all the weapons mentioned in this text. Which do you think was the worst? Explain your answer.

2 What do you think David Lloyd George meant when he said that General Haig was 'brilliant – to the top of his boots'?

3 Explain in your own words what the four expressions below mean.
over the top ____________________
no man's land ____________________
a wonder weapon ____________________
a black day ____________________

4 The main purpose of the songs sung by British soldiers was to:
a) frighten the Germans.
b) protest against the war.
c) make them fight more fiercely.
d) keep them cheerful.

Statue of General Haig

Red paper poppy

Section 2: *Topic development*

A Three war poets

One of the very few positive things to come out of the First World War was poetry. Many people believe that the 'war poets' wrote some of the finest poetry in the English language. Read the notes below about three of the best-known war poets. Then work with a partner to answer the questions that follow.

	Rupert Brooke 	Wilfred Owen 	Siegfried Sassoon 
Born	*1887*	*1893*	*1886*
Background	• *well-off academic family*	• *deeply religious English-Welsh family, struggled financially*	• *wealthy part-Jewish family*
Education and personality	• *went to Rugby School and Cambridge University* • *good student and athlete* • *popular* • *described as 'the handsomest young man in England'*	• *cheerful and optimistic when young* • *considered a career in the Church*	• *dropped out of Cambridge University to live the life of an English country gentleman, hunting, playing cricket and writing poetry*
War experience	• *saw little combat*	• *was blown up and also trapped underground for several days* • *treated for shell shock* • *went back to the war and fought bravely* • *awarded the Military Cross after his death*	• *earned the nickname 'Mad Jack' for his courage* • *awarded the Military Cross in 1916* • *wounded in April 1917* • *wrote an angry letter to The Times, criticizing the war leaders*
Died	• *1915, of blood poisoning resulting from a mosquito bite*	• *shot in the head on 4th November 1918, one week before the end of the war*	• *1967, after a long career as a leading English man of letters*
Poetry	• *expressed English patriotism and great enthusiasm for joining the war - saw it as a purifying force*	• *generally considered to be the greatest war poet - focused on the horrors of war*	• *angry about the war and satirized the officer class*

1 In every category, two of the poets have something in common. Say which is the odd one out in each case.

2 Match each poet to one of the examples of their poetry a)–c). (See *Tip!* below.)

3 Work in small groups. Practise reading the extracts aloud, paying attention to the rhyme and rhythm. Decide who reads the best in your group and choose one piece of poetry for him/her to read to the whole class. Help him/her to learn it by heart. The selected student can then present the poem to the class.

a)

Now, God be thanked who has matched us with His hour,
And caught our youth, and wakened us from sleeping,
With hand made sure, clear eye, and sharpened power,
To turn, as swimmers into cleanness leaping …

and

If I should die, think only this of me:
That there's some corner of a foreign field
That is forever England.

Poet: ______________________

b)

'Good-morning; good-morning!' the General said
When we met him last week on our way to the line.
Now the soldiers he smiled at are most of 'em dead
And we're cursing his staff for incompetent swine.

Poet: ______________________

c)

Men marched asleep. Many had lost their boots
But limped on, blood-shod. All went lame; all blind;
Drunk with fatigue; deaf even to the hoots
Of gas shells dropping softly behind.

Poet: ______________________

B Creatures as symbols

1 In the expression *lions led by donkeys, lions* represent courage and *donkeys* represent stubbornness and foolishness. Do they represent the same things in your culture?

2 Match the creatures 1–5 to what they represent in British culture, a)–e).

1 owl	a) fear, shyness
2 mouse	b) cunning
3 dog	c) strength, aggression
4 fox	d) wisdom
5 bear	e) faithfulness

Do the creatures 1–5 represent the same things in your culture? Work in pairs. Tell your partner about any different ideas these creatures represent. Then think of three more creatures and tell your partner what they symbolize for you.

TIP!

The language of poetry can be complex and there may be words you don't understand. So just try to get the general sense of the poems and find clues about who wrote them. Think about whether the writing is *patriotic* or *satirical*. Also consider what view of the war it is expressing.

Section 3: *Extension activities*

A Discuss

People thought that the First World War was so terrible that they called it the *Great War* and *The War to End All Wars*. However, the Second World War broke out only 20 years later. How do you think this was possible? Do human beings ever learn from history?

B Write

Write your own poem about war. It does not have to be about the First World War, but you can use vocabulary from the reading passage and from the poems opposite. It doesn't have to rhyme! (50+ words)

C Research

Search for: 'Tomb of the unknown warrior' + 'Westminster Abbey' + 'Christmas truce' + 'Tipperary' + 'A Long Way to Tipperary' + 'biggest British war cemetery' + 'Europe'

1 Find out about the tomb of the Unknown Warrior in Westminster Abbey, in London. Was the Unknown Warrior a real person?

2 Find out about the Christmas truce.
   - Which Christmas song did the British and German soldiers have in common?
   - Which sport united soldiers of both sides?
   - What does the Christmas truce tell you about the differences in attitude between the ordinary soldiers at the Front and their leaders?

3 *It's a Long Way to Tipperary* was a famous song of the First World War. Find out where Tipperary is. Then listen to the song online. Which two famous locations in London does it mention?

4 There are many British military cemeteries in France and Belgium. Find out which is the largest and where it is. Which battle scenes is it near? How many soldiers lie buried there?

9 Britain can take it: The Blitz

Section 1: *Reading*

A Before you read – think and discuss

The British people suffered greatly during the Blitz when some of the UK's cities came under attack from the German air force. However, the shared hardships of the time also brought people closer together.

- What difficult periods have there been in your country's history?
- What events have brought people in your country closer together?
- Who led your country through its most difficult times?
- What, if anything, do you know about the Blitz?

B Read the text

Britain can take it:

Churchill and the Blitz

Fact file

- 7th September 1940: the Blitz begins
- 16th May 1941: the Blitz ends
- 1940–41: 42,000 civilians killed
- 3.5 million houses destroyed in the same period
- Buckingham Palace suffers nine direct hits during the Blitz
- 10th May 1940: Winston Churchill becomes Prime Minister
- February 1945: German city of Dresden destroyed by the British Bomber Command

As I write, highly civilized human beings are flying overhead, trying to kill me.'

George Orwell, *England Your England*

The Blitz begins

During the Second World War, British cities came under German air attack in what came to be known as the Blitz. The name comes from the German word *Blitzkrieg* ('lightning war'), which described the rapid invasions of Poland in 1939 and France in 1940. The purpose of it was to wear down the morale of the British people. It began on 7th September 1940, when London was bombed, and ended on 16th May 1941 with an attack on Birmingham.

The bombing was focused on the capital from September to November 1940. It then switched to industrial centres like Coventry and Manchester, before moving to ports like Glasgow and Plymouth. When Hitler invaded the Soviet Union in the summer of 1941, German bombers turned their attention to the east of Europe. Nevertheless, attacks on Britain still took place. In 1942, historic cathedral cities such as York were bombed; and in 1944 London was hit by flying bombs (V-1s and V-2s, or 'doodlebugs').

Death and destruction

Economic and military targets were hit, but the main aim, to break the civilian population, failed completely. Nevertheless, there was a great deal of death and destruction. More civilians were killed in 1940–41 than British fighting men in the same period, and another 50,000 were seriously wounded.

Winston Churchill

Nevertheless, Winston Churchill's repeated **assertion** that 'Britain can take it' became the slogan that summed up the 'spirit of the Blitz'. Churchill had earlier saluted the brave airmen who defeated the Germans in the 'Battle of Britain' (August and September 1940) with the **stirring** words: 'Never in the field of human conflict was so much owed by so many to so few.' The Blitz, by contrast, was a story of *mass* resistance by the people themselves.

London's worst night

The worst raid on the capital occurred on the night of 29th December 1940. It caused what has been called the 'second Great Fire of London'. St Paul's Cathedral was in danger of being caught up in the flames but was saved, thanks to the constant efforts of firemen, **clergy** and local volunteers. This symbolized the resistance more than any other single event in the war. Despite the seriousness of this attack, ordinary citizens responded with remarkable bravery. When shop windows were broken or shops partly destroyed, owners wrote **witty** signs. 'If you think this is bad,' wrote one shopkeeper, 'you should see my branch in Berlin.' A message outside a badly damaged barber's shop read: 'Still open for business: a close shave.'

Bombed into democracy?

The working-class East End of London was most heavily bombed, because of the docks there. When a bomb landed on Buckingham Palace the Queen commented, 'At least now I can look the people of the East End in the face.' Some felt the Blitz was destroying Britain's class divisions along with its buildings. In 1941, a journalist wrote: 'Britain is being bombed, blasted and burnt into democracy.' But it is probably an exaggeration to say the Blitz transformed social relations. Whereas guests in London's Dorchester Hotel had silk sheets on the beds in their bomb shelters, residents in the poorest areas had no such luxuries. Some slept on the platforms of London Underground stations. Railway arches were also used as shelters – by as many as 15,000 people on bad nights. There were no toilets and these arches were often full of rats. It is perhaps no surprise then that six out of ten Londoners slept at home during the bombing.

Bomber Command

The Blitz created a powerful sense of national unity at a crucial point in the war. It also provided the moral **justification** for the Royal Air Force (RAF) to bomb German cities. 'Bomber' Harris was Commander-in-Chief of Bomber Command. He promised that because Germany had '**sown** the wind' it would now '**reap** the whirlwind'. The policy of bombing Germany ended on 14th February 1945, the day the beautiful German city of Dresden was destroyed.

Hero or criminal?

After the war, peace campaigners condemned Harris as a war criminal. They argued that there had been no strategic reason to bomb Dresden. While that was true, the RAF bombing did undermine German morale at a crucial late stage in the war and boost the British sense that they were finally gaining the upper hand. Harris asserted at the time that the cities of Germany were not worth the bones of a single British soldier. Most of Blitzed Britain agreed.

Glossary

assertion	claim
stirring	moving
clergy	churchmen
witty	clever and funny
justification	good reason for something that exists or has been done
sown*	planted
reap*	gather

*the saying *to reap what you sow* means something happens to you as a result of what you have done in the past

C Check your facts!

1 What made the Blitz different from *Blitzkriegs* in Europe?

2 The Blitz was aimed mainly at _____ targets.
a) military
b) economic
c) industrial
d) civilian

3 Did the Blitz kill more civilians or soldiers?

4 The Blitz and the Battle of Britain:
a) were two different names for the same thing.
b) were both inspirational events for the British.
c) both involved large numbers of British citizens.
d) brought the Second World War to a swift end.

5 What was the main danger to St Paul's Cathedral on 29th December 1940 – bombs or fire?

6 'Most Londoners sheltered in Tube stations during the Blitz.' True or false?

7 What two things does the author think the Blitz gave Britain in the Second World War?

8 'Most British people regarded Bomber Harris as a war criminal.' True or false?

D What do you think?

1 When Churchill described St Paul's as 'the parish church of Empire' he meant:
a) it was the whole Empire's beloved home church.
b) it was actually even bigger than a cathedral.
c) it was less important than people thought.
d) it was where people went to pray for the Empire.

2 Explain the double meaning in the notice outside the barber's shop: 'Still open for business: a close shave'.

3 The attitude of ordinary Londoners during the Blitz was:
a) mass panic.
b) witty defiance.
c) class prejudice.
d) a feeling of spreading democracy.

4 The Queen felt she could 'look the people of the East End in the face' because:
a) like the East Enders, her home had also been bombed.
b) she had been given a close shave by the royal barber.
c) she no longer slept on silk sheets in her bomb shelter.
d) the warm-hearted people there forgave her German origins.

5 Choose where a poor Londoner would be most likely to shelter during an attack.
a) Buckingham Palace
b) The Dorchester Hotel
c) under railway arches
d) Bomber Command
e) under a carpet bomb

Section 2: *Topic development*

A **Winston Churchill: The 'Greatest Briton'**

The BBC held a vote in 2002 to find the 'Greatest Briton' of all time. Winston Churchill, who led the country during World War II from 1940 until 1945, won easily. An aristocrat who enjoyed the good things in life, he had a long and colourful career, changing political parties twice. He warned against Hitler all through the 1930s, a 'voice in the wilderness' no one listened to. But his lasting fame comes from the way he led Britain through the darkest days of the war, with his fighting stance and inspirational speeches. He later wrote: 'It was a nation and race dwelling all around the globe that had the lion's heart. I had the luck to be called upon to give the roar'.

1 Work with a partner to match the events from Churchill's life below with the famous quotes on page 58. (One has been done for you as an example.)

Date	Event	Quote
Sep 1898	The young Churchill was a war correspondent in Africa and enthusiastically took part in one of the British Army's last cavalry charges.	
1904 + 1924	Churchill left the Conservative Party for the Liberals, then left the Liberals for the Conservatives again.	
13th May 1940	Churchill made his first speech to Parliament as wartime Prime Minister, warning members that the way ahead would be long and difficult and setting out Britain's war aims.	
4th June 1940	Churchill expressed Britain's spirit of defiance at a difficult point in the war.	
20th Aug 1940	Churchill praised the brave RAF pilots who had triumphed over Hitler and the German air force in the Battle of Britain.	j
9th Feb 1941	Churchill asked for America's help in the war – arms and money.	
8th May 1945	Churchill saluted victory over Germany in World War II.	
5th Mar	Stalin's USSR was taking over Eastern Europe.	
1946	Churchill championed the idea of European union in its early days.	
late 1940s	A female MP accused Churchill of being drunk.	

2 Now practise saying these quotes with your partner as you imagine Churchill might have said them. Think about speed, rhythm and intonation, and how loudly or quietly they should be spoken.

a) Give us the tools, and we will finish the job.

b) An iron curtain has descended across the continent.

c) We must build a kind of United States of Europe.

d) I have nothing to offer but blood, toil, tears and sweat ... You ask: 'What is our aim?' I can answer in one word: 'Victory!' Victory at all costs, victory in spite of terror, victory however long and hard the road may be: for without victory there is no survival.

e) There is nothing so exhilarating as being shot at without result.

f) A splendid moment both in our small lives and in our great history.

g) And you, madam, are ugly. But I shall be sober in the morning.

h) We shall defend our island, whatever the cost may be. We shall fight on the beaches, we shall fight on the landing grounds, we shall fight in the fields and in the streets, we shall fight in the hills: we shall never surrender.

i) I not only ratted but re-ratted.

j) Never in the field of human conflict was so much owed by so many to so few.

B The German invasion of English

English is partly a Germanic language. It has also imported many words from modern German (including *Blitz*).

1 Work with a partner to try to match the ten examples below with their meanings. Only use a dictionary if you are completely stuck.

kindergarten	a) broken, not working
delicatessen	b) a long kind of sausage
schadenfreude	c) a ghost that moves objects
angst	d) not the real thing, a low-quality substitute
frankfurter	e) a children's nursery
poltergeist	f) a recurrent theme in a work of art
kitsch	g) pleasure in the suffering of others
leitmotiv	h) low-quality art
ersatz	i) a shop selling cooked meats, cheeses, etc.
kaput	j) a strong feeling of anxiety

2 Discuss which of these words you like and which you don't. Give reasons – is it the sound or the look of it on the page? Do you know any words from your language which have entered English? If so, what are they? What about English words in your language?

3 Discuss: Should we try to protect our languages from foreign 'imports' like this, or is it better to be open, like English is, to words from other languages?

Section 3: *Extension activities*

A Discuss

At the end of the war, London was covered with bomb sites. What could be done with them?

In 1948, two young men bought a bomb site in Red Lion Square, Holborn, for £200. They made it into a car park. Within a decade they had a dozen city-centre car parks. In 1958, they took over National Car Parks (NCP), which they eventually sold for £580 million. Today NCP runs 500 car parks.

Brainstorm other ways of making money out of a big hole in the ground. Choose your favourite idea and make notes. Present your ideas to the class.

B Research

Search for: 'Churchill' + 'wartime speeches' 'fight them on the beaches' 'Murrow' + 'broadcasts'

1 Search the Internet for Winston Churchill's wartime speeches. Listen to some examples. What do you notice about his a) pronunciation and b) intonation?

2 Listen carefully to Churchill's famous 'We will fight them on the beaches' speech. Where does he say fighting will happen? Write down the places you hear.

3 Use the Internet to find out about Edward Murrow. He was an American journalist who broadcast directly from London during the Blitz, before the USA joined the Second World War. Why do you think his broadcasts had such a powerful impact on American public opinion in the period? Discuss your ideas.

C Write

During the Blitz, Noel Coward wrote the song *London Pride*. It is a song about the pride Londoners have in their city, and the resilient flower called London Pride. This flower bloomed during the Blitz, and grew in the ruins of the city's bombed buildings.

Search for the song *London Pride* on the Internet. Listen to the words. Now think about a city you love. Write a poem, story or song like *London Pride*. Celebrate your chosen city and remind people why they should be proud of it.

10 From the cradle to the grave: The welfare state

Section 1: *Reading*

A Before you read – think and discuss

Winston Churchill predicted that future generations would look back on Britain's resistance to Nazi Germany in the Second World War as the country's 'finest hour'. However, many view the creation of the welfare state after the war as an even greater achievement.

- Who gets special help from the state in your country?
- How much help do they get? Is it enough/more than enough?
- Do all the politicians agree about how much the state should help people?
- What, if anything, do you know about the British welfare state?

B Read the text

From the cradle to the grave: The welfare state

'This is the greatest advance in our history ... From now on Beveridge is not the name of a man; it is the name of a way of life, and not only for Britain, but for the whole civilized world.'

Harold Wilson (A young Harold Wilson made this statement in 1942. He was to become British Prime Minister from 1964–70 and from 1974–76.)

What is the UK's most important institution? A non-British person might answer Parliament, the civil service, the Church of England, the monarchy or even the BBC. But the average Briton would say the NHS (National Health Service). Whatever its failings, it is the institution that the British love above all others.

The NHS dates from July 1948. The work of Clement Attlee's Labour government (1945–51) in creating it and setting up the 'welfare state' is a defining event in modern British history. State-run services – in health, education, housing, social security and pensions – today take up about two-thirds of all government spending. At the start of the 20th century, none of these were provided by the state, except schooling up to age 12. But all that changed after the Second World War.

Governments of the Victorian era had a harsh attitude towards welfare. They feared that the poor would become dependent on government help instead of helping themselves. Local authorities ran workhouses for the poor, but their aim was as much to punish or **deter** poverty as to offer relief. They provided only the most basic support for those who simply could not survive on their own – the 'deserving' poor. The Victorians saw no reason for the state to take responsibility for the health or well-being of the 'undeserving' poor.

In the years before the First World War, Herbert Asquith's Liberal government felt the need to respond to the needs of an advanced industrial society. It included the **radical** Chancellor of the Exchequer David Lloyd George and the young Winston Churchill, who with certain other members of the cabinet came to be known as the 'New Liberals'. These men created the first-ever state-funded old age pensions as well as national insurance schemes to cover some workers against sickness and unemployment. While they arguably laid the foundations for the welfare state, they provided no more than a **means-tested** 'safety-net' for the most vulnerable.

But traditional thinking about welfare changed totally with the Second World War. It was the first 'people's war', and the key role played by civilians produced a social revolution. The economist Sir William Beveridge (1879–1963) is recognized as the founding father of the welfare state. His 1942 report was very much a product of its extraordinary times. Its aim was to look into existing social insurance arrangements and make recommendations for the future. Announcing his findings, he stated: 'The purpose of victory is to live in a better world than the old world.' He boldly claimed that the welfare state would '**slay** five giant evils' – Want, Disease, **Squalor**, Ignorance and **Idleness**. There was an ecstatic public response to the Beveridge report. One newspaper proclaimed that it would provide for people's vital needs 'from the cradle to the grave'.

The NHS was the centrepiece of Beveridge's scheme. Labour's formidable Health Secretary, Aneurin Bevan, was responsible for the detailed planning behind it. He met strong opposition from Britain's leading doctors, who were concerned about losing their independence and becoming state employees. In the end, Bevan effectively bought their support – 'I stuffed their mouths with gold,' he said. But the main beneficiaries of this bribery were the millions who until July 1948 were unable to afford basic treatment. In the first year of the NHS, for example, more than eight million pairs of free spectacles were ordered.

The post-war Labour government was also the first to commit itself to full employment. Social insurance became comprehensive rather than selective. **Compulsory** contributions to a national insurance scheme provided for incomes during sickness, unemployment, widowhood and retirement. There were child benefits and income support. For the first time, there was free secondary education for all. The government also began a massive house-building programme to deal with the homelessness caused by bomb damage.

Throughout the 1950s and 1960s there was cross-party consensus on the welfare state. Then in the 1970s right-wing politicians began to challenge this. As Margaret Thatcher stated, they were eager to 'roll back the frontiers of the state'. Their arguments, together with rising unemployment, raised concerns over costs and a 'dependency culture'. The election of Thatcher in 1979 put the very future of the welfare state in question. Her Conservative government sold over one million council houses to their tenants, and grew bolder in its approach after a third consecutive election victory in 1987. State education and the NHS continued, but there were increased state subsidies to the private alternatives. In addition, the Conservatives broke the link between pensions and earnings and cut the value of benefits to the unemployed. There was also a move towards a US-style 'workfare' system under which the unemployed lost the right to refuse jobs offered to them.

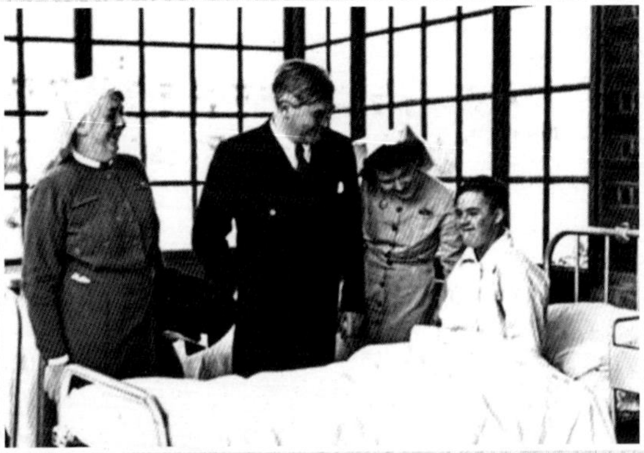

Bevan launches the NHS, 5th July 1948

Tony Blair's Labour government briefly promised profound changes to the welfare state after its massive victory in 1997. Blair delighted in challenging his own party's **'sacred cows'** and instructed one of his ministers, Frank Field, to 'think the unthinkable' on welfare reform. He did not get very far. Powerful opposition from his more traditional colleagues forced Field out of office after about a year. Despite the prime minister's wishes, the message could not be clearer: there would be little new thinking on welfare issues. Having set tough reforming standards, Blair clearly regretted the modesty of his government's record on welfare reform. The welfare state was still too obviously Beveridge's creation when he left office in June 2007. Although many British people were relieved about this, the Coalition government created in 2010 made simplifying the system of welfare payments a key priority. Its aim was to ensure that no one could receive more money from benefits than they could from working.

Glossary

deter	put off, discourage
radical	against tradition, wanting complete political or social change
means tested	based on a person's income
slay	kill
squalor	dirt, filth (especially in living conditions)
idleness	laziness, doing nothing, avoiding work
compulsory	forced, with no element of choice
sacred cows	most precious beliefs, above criticism

C Check your facts!

1 What is the UK's best-loved institution?
a) the BBC
b) the NHS
c) the welfare state
d) Parliament

2 'At the start of the 20th century, there were no state-run services.' True or false?

3 Victorian workhouses did **not** aim to _________ poverty.
a) punish
b) deter
c) relieve
d) support

4 Which group did the 'New Liberals' **not** help?
a) the old
b) the sick
c) the unemployed
d) the disabled

5 What was Sir William Beveridge by profession?
a) an economist
b) a politician
c) an announcer
d) a reporter

6 'Beveridge outlined the NHS but Bevan worked out the detail.' True or false?

7 Why was there a problem of homelessness in post-war Britain?

8 'The Conservative Party never accepted the welfare state.' True or false? Give reasons.

9 What prevented Tony Blair's Labour government from major reform of the welfare state?
a) unthinkable thoughts
b) the Conservative Party
c) sacred cows
d) traditional Labour MPs

D What do you think?

1 The 'deserving poor' are poor people who:
a) deserve to be poor.
b) deserve help from the state.

Explain your answer.

2 Explain in your own words what you understand the term 'safety net' to mean in the context of a welfare state.

3 Find a policy or an institution designed by the post-war Labour government to deal with:
a) want.
b) disease.
c) squalor.
d) ignorance.
e) idleness.

4 Explain your understanding of the term 'from the cradle to the grave'. Think of an alternative expression.

5 What did Mrs Thatcher have in common with the Victorians when it came to her fears about the state giving too much help to people?

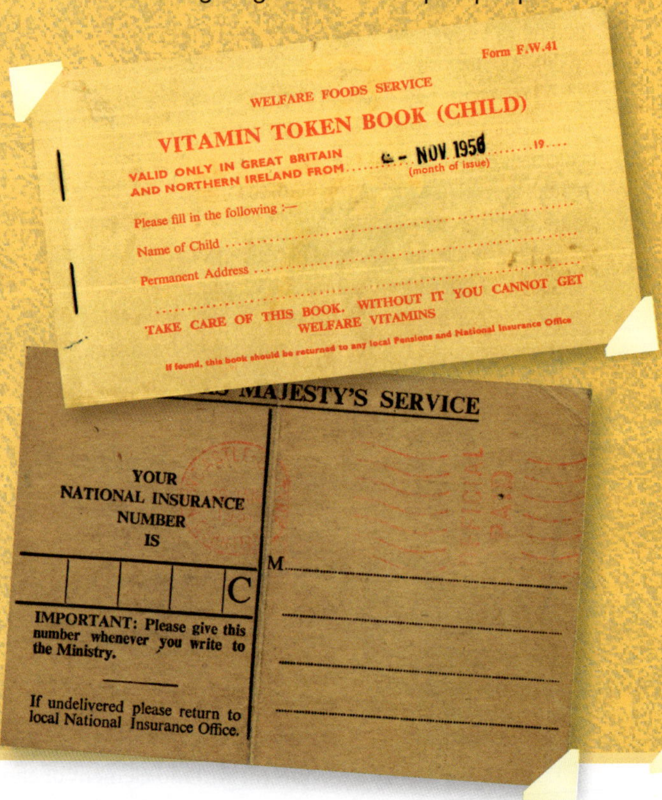

Section 2: *Topic development*

A Talking about our health

English uses a large number of expressions to talk about health.

1 Put the ones in the box below on a sliding scale from **100% healthy** to **nearly dead**. Three have been done for you as an example. Some of the expressions will go in the same place on the scale.

very run down   *coming down with something*   *in a very bad way*   *on the mend*
a bit under the weather   *at death's door*   *a picture of health*   *back on your feet*
mustn't grumble   *as right as rain*   *a bit off colour*   *out of sorts*

100% healthy	**OK**	**nearly dead**
as right as rain	*mustn't grumble*	*in a very bad way*

2 Now tell your partner(s) how you have been feeling this past month, using at least one of the expressions.

3 Is it polite to talk openly about your health in your culture? What do you think the British attitude is? (Give examples if possible.)

B NHS flowchart

1 Below is a flowchart of the possible stages a patient goes through when they see a doctor (or GP, 'general practitioner') about a medical problem. Five of the stages have been removed and put in random order beneath the chart. Work with a partner to put them in the correct boxes.

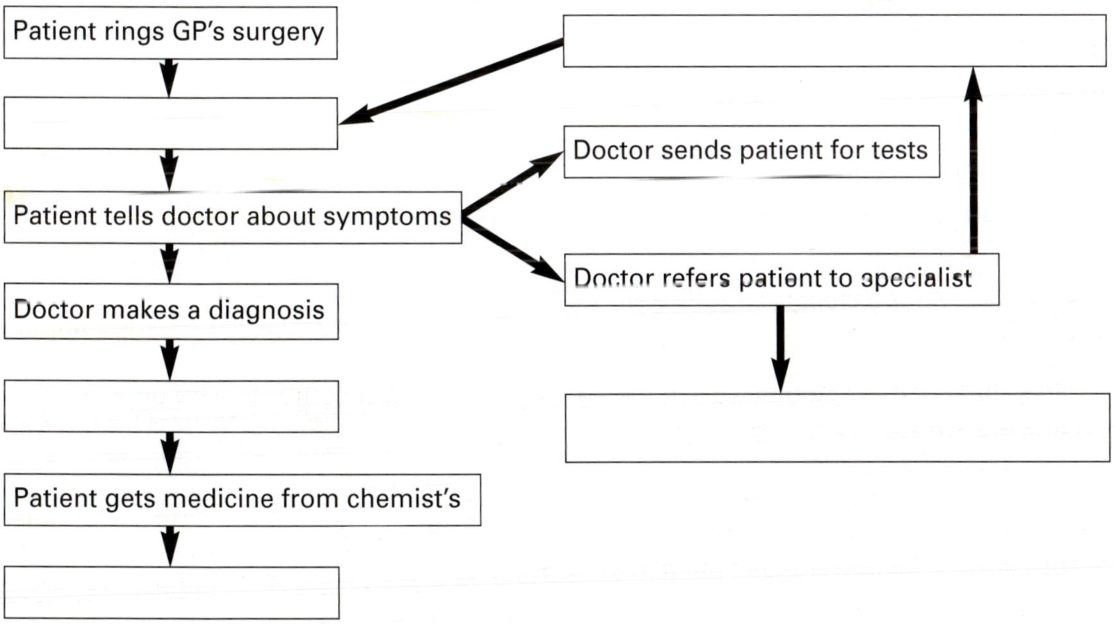

Specialist refers patient back to GP   *Patient takes prescribed course*
Patient speaks to receptionist and makes appointment
Patient has specialist treatment   *Doctor writes a prescription*

2 Now work with your partner to make a list of all the useful medical vocabulary in this exercise, e.g., *patient, GP, symptom*. Write your own simple definitions of these words.

3 Test another pair, giving your definitions and seeing if they can guess the word.

C Comparing welfare states

The UK was one of the first countries in the world to have a welfare state – people used to call it 'the envy of the world'. But many other countries have now caught up and overtaken the UK. Study the table below and answer the questions that follow.

nation	**welfare spend (% of GDP) minus education**	**welfare spend (% of GDP) with education**	**GDP per capita (US$)**
Sweden	28.9	38.2	$24,180
France	28.5	34.9	$23,990
Germany	27.4	33.2	$25,350
Italy	24.4	28.6	$24,670
United Kingdom	21.8	25.9	$24,160
Czech Republic	20.1	N/A	$14,720
Hungary	20.1	N/A	$12,340
Spain	19.6	25.3	$20,150
Australia	18.0	22.5	$25,370
Japan	16.9	18.6	$25,130
United States	14.8	19.4	$34,320
Ireland	13.8	18.5	$32,410
Mexico	11.8	N/A	$8,430
South Korea	6.1	11.0	$15,090

Source: OECD (2004), Social Expenditure Database (SOCX, www.oecd.org/els/social/expenditure)

1 Which country spends most of its GDP (= wealth) on welfare?

2 Which country spends most on education?

3 Which country spends least on education?

4 'The wealthier the country, the more it spends on welfare.' True or false?

Write three or more sentences comparing the UK with other countries. Use different comparative structures, e.g.,
The UK is richer/poorer than ...
The UK spends more/less on ... than ...
The UK spends a bigger/smaller proportion of its GDP on ... than ...
The UK is higher/lower in the table than ..., etc.

Section 3: *Extension activities*

A Discuss

Do you agree that the welfare state creates a 'dependency culture'? Discuss:

- who normally qualifies for benefits and why.
- what would happen to them if there were none.
- the advantages and disadvantages of a welfare state.
- what's wrong with people depending on the state.
- how you could improve the welfare state.

B Research

Search for: 'state pension' + 'history' + 'UK' 'William Beveridge' + 'last words' 'NHS' + 'number of employees' + 'annual budget'

1 Find out about the first state pension.
a) Who introduced it?
b) How much was it for?
c) Who qualified for it – how old were they and what did their income have to be?
d) What political crisis did it lead to in 1909–11?

2 Find out about William Beveridge.
a) When and where was he born?
b) When and where did he die?
c) Which political party did he belong to?
d) What were his last words?

3 Find out some key facts about the NHS.
a) How many employees does it have?
b) Which other organizations in the world employ more people?
c) What was the annual NHS budget last year?

C Write

Invent a new state benefit. Say:

- what it is called.
- who gets it and why.
- what the advantages are.
- where the money comes from to pay for it.
- how society as a whole might benefit.

(250 words)

11 Cultural revolution: The swinging sixties

Section 1: *Reading*

A Before you read – think and discuss

The 1960s is famous as a time of great social change in Britain. Many people feel that the country has not been the same since.

- What do we mean by social change – what kinds of things change?
- Has your country gone through a period of great social change in modern times?
- What happened in your country in the 1960s?
- What, if anything, do you know about Britain in the 1960s?

B Read the text

Cultural revolution: The swinging sixties

'The sixties saw an old world die and a new one come to birth.'
Bernard Levin (English journalist, author and broadcaster)

Historians often slice up the past into ten-year periods, each with its own distinct character. Arguably, there is no more colourful and vibrant decade in modern British history than the 1960s. This was a time of dramatic social change when, for good or ill, the country truly 'swung'.

At the start of the sixties, the Conservative Party was firmly in power. It had won a third consecutive general election in 1959, thanks mainly to the **consumer boom** celebrated in Prime Minister Harold Macmillan's slogan 'You've never had it so good'. But Macmillan's ageing government soon ran into trouble, appearing to be out of touch with unfolding social and cultural changes. This was made worse by the growing popularity of the Labour opposition leader, Harold Wilson. In a famous speech in 1963, he pledged his commitment to the 'white heat of the scientific revolution'. It would, he claimed, transform British society and industry for ever. The audience cheered, the press loved it and 'white heat' became a **catchphrase** for Labour's programme to modernize Britain.

For a brief period, Wilson seemed to be in complete control of everything. No British prime minister, until perhaps Tony Blair in 1997, has appeared so modern as Harold Wilson did in the mid-1960s. Today many may argue that his 1964–70 government failed to keep its promises, but it did bring about far-reaching changes in many areas of life. Spending on social services went up considerably, which meant that there was some redistribution of wealth. For the first time, there was real progress in making women's pay more equal to men's. In general, it was a time of **unprecedented** social mobility.

Wilson's government also reorganized secondary schooling. It had been the case that children sat an exam at the age of 11 to work out which school they should go to. In most parts of the country this system was replaced with 'comprehensive' schools, which were for pupils of all academic abilities. There was also a massive expansion of higher education, with the founding of 22 new universities. Thousands of young people whose parents would never have dreamed of going to university were now able to gain degrees. In 1969, Wilson set up the Open University, a unique distance learning institution open to all.

Roy Jenkins was the Labour government's reforming home secretary and he was responsible for the acceleration of social change. He abolished **capital punishment** and liberalized the law on abortion, homosexuality and divorce. Previously, abortion had been illegal and unmarried mothers had suffered social disapproval and rejection. In turn, this had resulted in a high number of **'backstreet' abortions**. Homosexuality had been a crime as well as a social taboo. It had ruined careers and quite often led to blackmail, but the law now allowed for same-sex relationships 'between consenting adults over 21'.

Perhaps inevitably, there was a powerful **backlash** against the new 'permissive society'. Church leaders often tried to 'understand' the younger generation, but many newspapers carried angry criticism of social change. This mood was most forcibly expressed by a schoolteacher from the Midlands called Mary Whitehouse. Her National Viewers' and Listeners' Association aimed to push the media (especially the BBC) into cleaning up the 'moral filth' they thought was poisoning the airwaves.

Most of the really interesting developments of the 1960s took place away from Westminster politics. In London, the King's Road and Carnaby Street were meeting places for young people who were developing a very distinctive culture. Their attitude was summed up by the designer Mary Quant, whose shop in the King's Road provided clothes that allowed people 'to run, to jump, to leap, to retain their precious freedom'. A key symbol of social change was music. No band was more influential than The Beatles, the most successful

pop group of all time. Formed in Liverpool in the late 1950s, The Beatles had their first British Number One hit in May 1963 with the song *From Me to You*. 'Beatlemania' swept the country, powered by the band's good looks, dynamism and catchy tunes. Combining youth rebellion with commercialism, they gave teenagers an identity that cut across class, accent and region.

The sixties' cultural revolution peaked in 1968, the 'year that rocked the world'. Anti-nuclear and anti-Vietnam War protests led to huge demonstrations outside the US Embassy in London's Grosvenor Square, involving 100,000 people. Radios played protest songs by Bob Dylan and The Rolling Stones. There was hardly a student in the land who did not have a poster of South American revolutionary Che Guevara on the bedroom wall. Strongly influenced by the wave of student unrest which had begun in Paris in May, a number of student groups staged sit-ins at their colleges.

There are many myths about the 1960s, and there is truth in the view that the decade was in fact as much about tradition as change. To take one small example: the biggest-selling album was not by The Beatles but was, in fact, the soundtrack to the family musical *The Sound of Music*. Yet many still see the period as a vital flowering of freedom and self-expression. Its inspiration was the firmly held (if perhaps naïve) belief that, as The Beatles sang, 'All You Need Is Love'.

Glossary

consumer boom	time of growing wealth when people buy more
catchphrase	well-known phrase or slogan
unprecedented	not seen before
capital punishment	putting to death by the state
'backstreet' abortion	an illegal abortion carried out by an untrained person, often in dirty conditions
backlash	strong negative reaction

C Check your facts!

1 The 1960s were **not**:
a) colourful.
b) conservative.
c) distinct.
d) dramatic.

2 'Harold Macmillan's government ran into trouble after 1959 because it was young and inexperienced.' True or false?

3 Harold Wilson was prime minister:
a) until 1997.
b) in the mid-1960s.
c) from 1964 to1970.
d) throughout the 1960s.

4 How many universities did Harold Wilson's government set up?

5 What did Roy Jenkins abolish?
a) abortion
b) divorce
c) capital punishment
d) homosexuality

6 The backlash against the 1960s permissive society was led by:
a) the Church.
b) newspapers.
c) schoolteachers.
d) Mary Whitehouse.

7 'The Beatles were a product of London in the 1960s.' True or false?

8 What were people demonstrating against in Grosvenor Square in 1968?

9 '*All You Need Is Love* was the best-selling album of the 1960s.' True or false?

D What do you think?

1 Which groups in society 'had it good' in the 1960s?

2 'Macmillan had no feeling for the developing consumer society that marked the 1960s.' True or false? Give reasons.

3 When Harold Wilson spoke of 'the white heat of the scientific revolution', he was promising:
a) a general switch from gas to electricity.
b) more 'white goods' – fridges, freezers, etc.
c) a super-fast hi-tech transformation.
d) a warm, light country – not a dark, cold one.

4 How did the media influence change? Give an example each for:
a) radio.
b) TV.
c) newspapers.

5 What kind of clothes do you think Mary Quant meant when she said they allowed people 'to run, to jump, to leap, to retain their precious freedom'? Give examples.

Section 2: *Topic development*

A Sixties slang

The youth culture of the 1960s produced its own slang, some of which is still in use today.

1 As it was an optimistic decade, there were a lot of words and phrases expressing positive approval. Not everything was wonderful, however, and there were also some negative ones. Work with a partner to put the eight below in the right box, using a dictionary if you need to.

a gas **fab** **a drag** **a bummer** **far out** **groovy** **heavy** **hip**

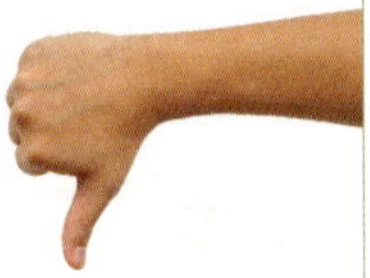

2 To **go ape** and to **hang loose** are both well-known sixties expressions, with more or less opposite meanings. Which one means a) to explode with anger, and b) to relax and take things easy?

3 Work with a partner to match the following sixties slang expressions to their meanings (think about what kind of word it is – noun, verb? – and what it suggests). One has been done for you as an example.

bread	spots (on skin)
a chrome dome	go to bed; go to sleep
a pad →	money
zits	→ someone's house
to crash	someone who only thinks about money
a bread-head	a bald man

4 Discuss which words and phrases you like/don't like – and why. Do you think you might use any of them in your English? In which situations could you use them?

5 Now prepare a short '1960s dialogue' with your partner(s). Write it down and practise it together. Your teacher will choose the best one(s) and ask the students to perform to the class.

B The 11-plus

Before the educational reforms of the 1960s, all 11-year-olds had to take this selective exam. The minority who passed went to the best, 'grammar' schools. Work with a partner to answer the questions on page 70, taken from an old 11-plus General English paper, then move on to the follow-up discussion tasks.

1 Make adjectives from these nouns: beauty, slope, glass, friend, doubt, expense, delight, sleep, danger, sport.

2 Choose the correct word from those in brackets:

a) She gave the (fare, fair) to the conductor.

b) I am (confidant, confident) of success.

c) Why does she (die, dye) her hair?

d) His sister has (wrote, written) him a letter.

e) The screw fell off because it was (lose, loose).

3 Each of the following sentences contains one error. Re-write the sentences correctly:

a) This is not an Infant's School.

b) I am told that Tom Jones's brother have won a scholarship.

c) When the dog recognised me it wagged it's tail.

d) The matter does not concern you or I.

e) Talking to my friend, the bus passed me.

1 Did you find these questions easy or difficult?
2 Do you think today's 11-year-olds could answer them?
3 Is it a good idea to divide children on the basis of academic ability at the age of 11?
4 Why do you think the government wanted to end selective education in the 1960s?
5 Do you think it would be better for Britain to go back to this selective system? Why/why not?

C Sad poet

Not everyone felt part of the 1960s. The English poet Philip Larkin thought that he was just a little too old. Read the extract from his poem *Annus Mirabilis* below, using the rhymes to put the four words below in the correct place, then answer the questions that follow.

me	game	three	became

Everyone felt the same,
And every life ______
A brilliant breaking of the bank,
A quite unlosable ____.

So life was never better than
In nineteen sixty-_____
(Though just too late for _____)

1 What does the Latin expression *Annus Mirabilis* in the title mean? (Check in a dictionary if necessary.)
2 Which specific year does Larkin mention? Given that he was born in 1922, how old would he have been then?
3 How does this poetry make you feel? Discuss with your partner(s).
4 Would you have enjoyed the 1960s, or do you think you would have felt left out like Larkin?

Section 3: *Extension activities*

A Discuss

Is there anything wrong with the idea that 'All You Need Is Love'? Discuss:

- what you think it actually means.
- what the dangers are of such a belief, if any.
- if you think the 1960s really were all about love.
- the relevance of such a message today.

B Research

Search for: 'The Beatles' 'The Rolling Stones' '1960s fashions' + 'miniskirt' + 'bell-bottoms' + 'tie-dye' + 'go-go boots' 'England' + 'World Cup winners'

1 What do you know about The Beatles and The Rolling Stones?
  a) Where and when were they formed?
  b) How does their music differ?
  c) Who are/were their most famous members?
  d) What tragedies have affected the bands?
  e) Who broke up first?

2 Find out about these sixties fashions:
  a) miniskirts
  b) bell-bottoms
  c) tie-dye clothes
  d) go-go boots

  What were all these fashion items? Who wore them? Do you like them?

C Write

Do you think the social changes of the 1960s were mainly good or bad? Consider:

- what changed.
- how things are different today because of those changes.
- how things were before.
- what you think the mistakes of the 1960s were.
- what you like about the 1960s – music, fashion, politics, etc.

(250 words)

12 The Iron Lady: Margaret Thatcher

Section 1: *Reading*

A Before you read – think and discuss

Margaret Thatcher is the only female prime minister in British history. Many countries have never had a woman as a leader.

- Has your country ever had a female leader?
- What other countries have had female leaders?
- What, if anything, do you know about Margaret Thatcher and the way she changed Britain?

B Read the text

THE IRON LADY

'If you lead a country like Britain, a strong country, a country which has taken a lead in world affairs in good times and in bad, a country that is always reliable, then you have to have a touch of iron about you.'
Margaret Thatcher

Margaret Thatcher is probably the most significant British political figure of the post-1945 period. She was not only Britain's first woman prime minister, but also Britain's only 20th-century leader to win three general elections in a row. The force of her personality defined much of the 1980s and was felt way beyond Britain's borders. When she came to power in 1979 she promised to bring harmony, but in fact her rule was marked by deep divisions and unrest.

Margaret Thatcher was a grocer's daughter and her outlook on life was strongly influenced by her father's belief in **thrift** and hard work. She once explained what she had learnt at his knee: 'His simple conviction that some things were right, and some are wrong. His belief that life is ultimately about character, that character comes from what you make of yourself, but hard work was even more important in the formation of character. You must learn to stand on your own two feet.'

She led the Conservative Party to power in May 1979 after the 'Winter of Discontent', a period of growing unemployment and angry strikes. Before coming to power, she already had a reputation for doing things her way. As Education Secretary in the 1970–74 Conservative government, she had cut free school milk for eight- to eleven-year-olds. This earned her the nickname 'Thatcher the Milk Snatcher'. Some people saw the views she expressed before becoming prime minister as racist. For example, she once said that many British people felt **swamped** by large-scale immigration. From an early stage it was clear that she thought of her political career as a crusade – a battle between right and wrong – with no room for compromise.

By 1981, opinion polls showed that she was the most unpopular prime minister since records began. Unemployment had reached close to three million as a direct result of her radical economic policies. In the meantime, despite her government's attempts to control it, inflation continued to rise. That summer, there were violent riots in the inner-city areas of London, Liverpool and Bristol, and there was enormous pressure on her to do a U-turn. But she remained true to her previously stated beliefs: 'To those waiting with bated breath for that famous media catchphrase, the U-turn, I have only this to say: You turn if you want; the lady's not for turning.'

The invasion of the Falkland Islands by Argentina in April 1982 gave Mrs Thatcher a powerful diversion from Britain's domestic problems, and the opportunity to confirm her reputation as a strong leader. Britain's quick victory in the Falklands War greatly strengthened her position and gave the impression that she could not be beaten. Large Conservative victories followed in the general elections of 1983 and 1987, by which time the economic clouds had lifted for most people.

During Mrs Thatcher's time in office, there were many significant reforms. These had a lasting effect on British society and the economy. Her stated aim was to 'roll back the frontiers of the state' and make socialism history. Her government sold over one million state-owned council houses to private buyers and privatized major state-owned businesses such as gas, electricity and the telephone network. It also greatly reduced the trade union power that had been a key factor in the **turbulent** politics of the previous two decades. Trade unions could no longer force workers to belong to them or call a strike without a secret **ballot** of workers; and it was now against the law for sympathetic workers to join strikes in other industries. In 1984–85, Mrs Thatcher defeated Britain's most powerful union, the National Union of Mineworkers, in one of the most bitter and violent industrial disputes in the country's history.

However, by the late 1980s, Thatcher's rule was becoming increasingly **authoritarian** and **eccentric**. This made even her strongest supporters less loyal. The introduction of the 'poll tax' in 1989 in the teeth of fierce

opposition and her increasing hostility towards Europe were important factors in her downfall. She was finally driven from office in November 1990, not by her opponents or **the electorate**, but by her own party. In a leadership contest, Conservative MPs voted to replace her with John Major. The Iron Lady left Downing Street for the final time with tears in her eyes and a burning sense of betrayal.

Thatcherism claimed that everyone would benefit if government promoted individual self-interest and that wealth would start to trickle down from rich to poor. Mrs Thatcher once said that there was 'no such thing as society. There are individual men and women, and there are families.' Her political aim was a clear attempt to return to the values of the Victorian era, when Britain was at the height of its power and wealth. But in the 1980s, these values often led to consumerist greed and dishonest dealing rather than the thrift and morality that Mrs Thatcher championed.

Glossary

thrift	being careful with money
swamped	flooded
turbulent	rough, unsettled
ballot	vote
authoritarian	bossy, controlling
eccentric	odd, strange
the electorate	the voters

C Check your facts!

1 What two facts allow us to claim that Mrs Thatcher is probably the most significant British prime minister post-1945?

2 Mrs Thatcher's father was:
a) a milkman.
b) a politician.
c) a teacher.
d) a grocer.

3 Did Mrs Thatcher coming to power cause the 'Winter of Discontent'?

4 Which of the following decreased during Mrs Thatcher's first two years as prime minister?
a) inflation
b) her popularity
c) unemployment
d) street violence

5 What was the main effect of the Falklands War for Mrs Thatcher?

6 Which of the following did Mrs Thatcher's government **not** privatize?
a) gas
b) electricity
c) trade unions
d) council houses
e) the telephone network

7 Who got rid of Mrs Thatcher in the end?
a) her own party
b) the National Union of Mineworkers
c) the European Union
d) eccentric opponents

8 'Mrs Thatcher believed that families were more important than society.' True or false?

D What do you think?

1 Is it fair to say that Mrs Thatcher was able to bring harmony to Britain? Explain your answer.

2 Mrs Thatcher said she had learnt things at her father's knee. This means:
a) she learnt things when she was a young child.
b) that he knelt down to teach her things.
c) she learnt things when she sat on his lap.
d) that he couldn't stand on his own two feet.

3 Make a list of everything and anything, at home and abroad, that Mrs Thatcher was hostile to.

4 When Mrs Thatcher said 'the lady's not for turning', she was talking about:
a) the Queen of the United Kingdom.
b) herself as prime minister of Britain.
c) a British warship heading for the Falklands.

5 Some people argue that, in the end, everyone got rich in Mrs Thatcher's Britain. Do you believe that they did? Explain your answer.

Section 2: *Topic development*

A Thatcher idioms

1 Match idioms a)–c) with pictures 1–3.

a) to do a U-turn ___

b) the economic clouds had lifted ___

c) to trickle down ___

1

2

3

2 What do these body idioms mean? Discuss your ideas with a partner.

a) to stand on your own two feet

b) to wait with bated breath

c) to do something in the teeth of fierce opposition

3 Discuss with a partner any **three** of the following.

- Have you ever had to **perform a U-turn** in life? Why? What happened?
- Do you believe that wealth **trickles down** from the rich to the poor? Give examples.
- What **economic clouds** are there at the moment?
- When did you first have to **stand on your own two feet**?
- Are you **waiting with bated breath** for something at the moment? What is it?
- Have you ever done something **in the teeth of fierce opposition**? What was it? Did you succeed?

4 Mrs Thatcher made the speech below the day after she was elected prime minister. She quoted from St Francis of Assisi, a Christian saint who lived over 800 years ago. Complete the speech by matching the words in bold with their opposites. Use the words in the box.

faith	harmony	hope	truth

Where there is **discord**, may we bring _______.

Where there is **error**, may we bring _______.

Where there is **doubt**, may we bring _______.

And where there is **despair**, may we bring _______.

B Thatcher quotes

1 Complete the quotes using the words in the box.

consensus	done	economic	evasive	heaven	history	home	nuclear	said	swim

a) *On being a leader:* *'To me, __________ seems to be the process of abandoning all beliefs, principles, values and policies. So it is something in which no one believes and to which no one objects.'*

b) *On the work ethic:* *'Pennies do not come from __________. They have to be earned here on Earth.'*

c) *On economics:* *'There can be no liberty unless there is __________ liberty.'*

d) *On history:* *'Europe was created by __________. America was created by philosophy.'*

e) *On world peace:* *'A world without __________ weapons would be less stable and more dangerous for all of us.'*

f) *On dealing with critics:* *'If my critics saw me walking over the Thames they would say it was because I couldn't __________.'*

g) *On diplomacy:* *'You don't tell deliberate lies, but sometimes you have to be __________.'*

h) *On being a woman:* *'Any woman who understands the problems of running a __________ will be nearer to understanding the problems of running a country.'*

i) *On male–female differences:* *'If you want anything __________, ask a man. If you want something __________, ask a woman.'*

2 Which of the quotes above do you agree with? Which do you disagree with? Discuss in pairs.

Section 3: *Extension activities*

A Discuss

What do you think would be different if women had ruled the world's leading countries for the last 500 years? In groups, discuss whether the world would be more or less:

- authoritarian.
- competitive.
- equal.
- logical.

B Research

Search for: 'Spitting Image' + 'Thatcher' + 'video'   'Thatcher and Gorbachev' + 'Pravda' + 'Iron Lady' + 'fall of Berlin Wall'

1 Search the Internet for examples of how the satirical TV programme *Spitting Image* portrayed Mrs Thatcher during the 1980s. Make notes about and discuss whether you think:
- the programme-makers were fair to Mrs Thatcher.
- satire* is part of a healthy political environment.

*the use of humour to criticize someone

2 Does satire like this exist in your country? (If not, how would people react to it?)

3 Find out about Margaret Thatcher's relationship with President Gorbachev of the USSR.
a) What did she think of him?
b) What did he think of her?
c) How did the Soviet press describe her?
d) How did they both view the fall of the Berlin Wall?

The 2012 film *The Iron Lady*, starring Meryl Streep, was a big success and won many awards. However, not everyone approved of the film. Find out what the main criticisms were.

C Write

Imagine you have just been made leader of your country. You have to make a short speech, like Mrs Thatcher did when she talked about bringing harmony, truth, faith and hope. Write a speech saying what you would like to bring to your people. (250 words)

TIP! **Think about what you don't like about your country and how you could make it better.**

13 FROM BARONS TO BALLOT BOX: THE LONG ROAD TO DEMOCRACY

Section 1: *Reading*

A Before you read – think and discuss

The British people have been challenging power for many centuries. Despite this, the ability for everyone to vote has been in place for less than a century.

- What is democracy?
- Is it appropriate for all countries?
- Have there been struggles for democracy in your country?
- What, if anything, do you know about British democracy?

The signing of the Magna Carta

B Read the text

File Edit View Favorites Tools Help

FROM BARONS TO BALLOT BOX:
THE LONG ROAD TO DEMOCRACY

'Democracy is the worst form of government except all those other forms that have been tried from time to time.' Winston Churchill

Fact file
- 1066: Normans conquer Britain
- 1215: Signing of Magna Carta. Some of King John's power given over to his barons
- 1649: Execution of Charles I
- 1660: Restoration of the monarchy
- 1688–89: Glorious Revolution: establishes Bill of Rights
- 1832: Great Reform Act: gives vote to about 20 per cent of male population
- 1867: Reform Act: widens vote to skilled working man
- 1913: Suffragette throws herself under the King's horse
- 1914–18: World War I
- 1918: Women over 30 and working-class men get the vote through the Representation of the People Act
- 1928: Women get equal voting rights to men

How old is democracy in Britain?

Many British people take pride in a democracy based on a 1,000-year-old monarchy and a Westminster Parliament dating back eight centuries. But full democracy in Britain is not really so ancient. Working-class men and some middle-class women first gained the right to vote in 1918. Women have only voted on equal terms with men since 1928. By contrast, the struggle for democratic representation and guaranteed legal rights is truly ancient. It drew strength from the belief that pre-1066, Anglo-Saxons had lived as free and equal citizens who stayed loyal to the king only if he ruled well.

The Norman legacy

People thought that the Normans who conquered England in that year had deprived these 'freeborn Englishmen' of their rights and liberties. Many even viewed the Magna Carta as a deal which gave little to the monarch's ordinary subjects. Yet generations of reformers have gained inspiration from this famous **charter**, which affirmed the right of 'the people' to force over-mighty rulers like King John to share power.

Democracy and the monarchy

In the mid-17th century, Britain seemed to cast off the so-called 'Norman Yoke' forever. Civil war led to the execution of the **absolutist** King Charles I in 1649. This revolutionary act gave rise to a unique episode of republican rule under Oliver Cromwell and then briefly his son Richard. For 11 years anything seemed possible, even what some radicals proposed: full democracy based on one man (if not one person), one vote. The return of the monarchy in 1660 under Charles II – and then his brother, the absolute monarch James II – set the democratic clock firmly back. But not for long. The Glorious Revolution of 1688–89 ('glorious' because non-violent) established a **constitutional monarchy** and a **Bill of Rights**. In the decades that followed, it was clear that real political power in England now lay with MPs and Lords at Westminster rather than the monarch, whose role became mostly ceremonial.

Widening the democratic franchise

From the late 18th century, the pursuit of democracy centred on attempts to widen the **franchise** for elections to the House of Commons. It proved to be a long, hard struggle. Reformers battled with a ruling class who thought giving the vote to more people would lead to 'mob rule'. The ruling class had been made especially fearful by the violent revolutions in France and America, which undoubtedly inspired some radicals. The Great Reform Act followed widespread popular unrest and gave the vote to the middle classes only, extending it to about 20 per cent of the male population. Frustration with the limited nature of this act inspired the Chartist movement, the largest working-class organization in British history, which demanded votes for all adult men. The Reform Act of 1867 **enfranchised** the skilled working classes but still left a large majority of men without the vote. Nevertheless, it changed the nature of politics forever. Politicians now had to work much harder to win their voters' approval at election time. Party organization was tighter and campaigns more professional. The introduction of the secret ballot in 1872 greatly reduced electoral corruption. Many historians argue that this period, the age of Gladstone and Disraeli, marked the birth of modern politics.

In the years before the First World War (1914–18), female **suffrage** campaigners rocked the British political establishment. These Suffragettes occupy an iconic position in 20th-century British history. They argued that struggle using peaceful means did not work and pursued their aims with angry passion. They set fire to public buildings, horsewhipped Cabinet ministers, smashed windows, chained themselves to railings, went on hunger strike, blew up postboxes and slashed paintings in galleries. One Suffragette was trampled to death in 1913 after she deliberately ran into the path of a racehorse owned by King George V. But there was more to the Suffragettes than violence. Christabel Pankhurst, the movement's leader, spoke for generations of male and female campaigners for democracy when she declared, 'We are here, not because we are law-breakers; we are here in our efforts to become law-makers.'

Towards full democracy

Though the Suffragette movement no longer existed, a minority of British women got the vote when the war ended, through the Representation of the People Act. Full democracy, once achieved, proved to be impressively **robust**. During the interwar era, most of Europe fell under extremist regimes. But in this age of dictators, British politics remained stubbornly moderate. Under the leadership of three successive prime ministers, Ramsay MacDonald, Stanley Baldwin and Neville Chamberlain, democracy prevailed. During the 1920s and 1930s, not a single fascist and only one communist was elected to Parliament.

Democracy's 'finest hour'

Arguably, British democracy's 'finest hour' came just after the Second World War ended in Europe. Although the vast majority of the country admired Winston Churchill for his inspiring war leadership, he failed to persuade voters that he was the right man to lead them in peacetime. The Labour Party and its leader, Clement Attlee, humiliated his government in the 1945 election. It was a triumph for policies over personality and sentiment. As far as voters were concerned, the country's future needs were more important than its past glories. Churchill had been a great warrior for democracy. The irony was that democracy, not Adolf Hitler, proved to be his downfall.

Glossary

charter	a written statement of the rights of a particular group
absolutist	believing in royal power without limits (see Chapter 5)
constitutional monarchy	a monarchy limited by law and custom
Bill of Rights	a written statement of the rights of the people
franchise	the right to vote in public elections
enfranchised	having the right to vote
suffrage	the right to vote in political elections
robust	strong

C Check your facts!

1 When did Britain become a full democracy?

2 'Free-born Englishmen' refers to:
a) Normans after the Magna Carta.
b) Anglo-Saxons before the Norman Conquest.
c) barons after the reign of King John.
d) King John's men before Magna Carta.

3 'The period of republican rule that followed the execution of King Charles I led to one man, one vote.' True or false?

4 'Despite the reforms of 1832 and 1867, only a minority of British men had the vote.' True or false?

5 Which of the following was **not** a form of Suffragette protest?
a) smashing windows
b) trampling to death
c) going on hunger strike
d) slashing paintings

6 'The Representation of the People Act in 1918 meant that all women had the right to vote.' True or false?

7 Churchill lost the 1945 election because of:
a) his war leadership.
b) his support for democracy.
c) Attlee's charisma.
d) Labour's better policies.

D What do you think?

1 Name five important milestones on 'the long road to democracy' in Britain.

2 What is the main difference between a constitutional monarchy and an absolute monarchy?

3 Choose the best summary of this statement: 'We are here, not because we are law-breakers; we are here in our efforts to become law-makers.'
a) We want the law to change so that our activities are legal.
b) We are in trouble because of our illegal law-making.
c) We break the law because we want political power.
d) We haven't broken the law but are trying to mend it.

4 What helped women eventually to get the vote?

5 By pointing out that not a single fascist and only one communist was elected to Parliament, the author is trying to say that Britain:
a) was more communist than fascist.
b) was not politically extreme.
c) had an unfair voting system.
d) did not represent all views.

Section 2: *Topic development*

A Understanding legal language: *Habeas Corpus*

Habeas Corpus is a Latin term whose literal meaning is 'you may have the body'. It is based on two articles of the Magna Carta and is a fundamental principle of English law.

Read the two articles below and work with a partner to answer the questions that follow. (Don't worry if you can't understand it all – most native speakers also have problems with legal language!)

Article 38 *In future no official shall place a man on trial upon his own unsupported statement, without producing credible witnesses to the truth of it.*

Article 39 *No free man shall be seized or imprisoned, or stripped of his rights or possessions, or outlawed or exiled, or deprived of his standing in any other way, nor will we proceed with force against him, or send others to do so, except by the lawful judgment of his equals or by the law of the land.*

1 Match the two brief summaries below to Article 38 and Article 39.
  a) No trial without evidence and witnesses.
  b) No prison or punishment without a legal trial.

2 Do you think these are good principles? What happens if they are not followed?

3 Do you think these principles of English law are still applied today in all appropriate situations? Give reasons and examples if possible.

B A Suffragette poster

1 Study this Suffragette poster from 1912, and match the different things that women and men may be with the pictures.

lunatic convict mother drunkard mayor proprietor of white slaves
doctor or teacher unfit for service factory hand nurse

FROM BARONS TO BALLOT BOX: THE LONG ROAD TO DEMOCRACY

2 Are the things men may be mainly positive or negative?

3 Are the things women may be mainly positive or negative?

4 Explain in no more than 20 words what you think the message of this poster is.

5 Discuss the difference between *may be* and *maybe* in this sentence:

A woman may be a mother and maybe also have a profession.

C Not in their name

A 1913 poster supporting votes for women carried the name of the President of the National Union of Women's Suffrage Societies (NUWSS) at the top: 'Mrs Henry Fawcett'. She had been born Millicent Garrett, but changed her name on marrying Henry Fawcett in 1867. He died in 1884.

1 What does this tell you about the custom for married women's names at the time?

2 What about widows?

3 What does it tell you about the NUWSS? How strongly feminist do you think it was?

4 How does this custom compare with your own country's customs?

5 Do you think most British women still take their husband's first and second names like Mrs Henry Fawcett? Give reasons or examples.

6 Discuss what the titles below tell us about a woman's marital status.

a) Mrs
b) Miss
c) Ms

Which one should you use if you are not sure about a woman's marital status?

Section 3: *Extension activities*

A Discuss

Discuss Churchill's statement that 'Democracy is the worst form of government except all those other forms that have been tried from time to time.'

- What did he mean?
- What other forms of government are there?
- What are their advantages and disadvantages?
- What are the advantages and disadvantages of democracy?
- Do you agree with Churchill? Why?

B Research

Search for: 'Mother of Parliaments' / 'Magna Carta' + 'surviving copies' / 'first woman elected to Parliament'

1. Find out about the origin of the phrase 'the Mother of Parliaments'.
   - Who was originally supposed to have said it?
   - When?
   - Were they quoted correctly?
   - If not, what did they actually say?
2. Find out about surviving copies of the Magna Carta.
   - How many 1215 originals are left in Britain today?
   - Where are they?
   - Which American politician owns a later copy?
   - Where else could you see a later copy?
3. Find out about the first woman to be elected to Parliament.
   - Who was she?
   - Which party did she represent?
   - Had she been involved in the struggle for women's suffrage?
   - Was she the first woman to sit in Parliament? Why/why not?

C Write

Do you think it is ever acceptable for people to break the law to advance a cause they believe in? Include:

- the kinds of action people take to advance their cause.
- what the consequences can be.
- what the dangers are.
- whether you think there is any justification – and in what circumstances.
- whether any good comes from such actions. (250 words)

14 The Bard of Avon: William Shakespeare

Section 1: *Reading*

A Before you read – think and discuss

William Shakespeare is the greatest of English writers, yet we know very little about his life.

- Who is considered to be your country's greatest writer?
- What do you know about him/her?
- Is it important to know the life story of great writers?
- What do you know about Shakespeare and his work?

B Read the text

File Edit View Favorites Tools Help

The Bard* of Avon: William Shakespeare

*poet

'He was not a man, he was a continent; he contained whole crowds of great men, entire landscapes.' ***Gustave Flaubert***

Fact file

- 26th April 1564: William Shakespeare born in Stratford-upon-Avon.
- Late 1580s or early 1590s: Shakespeare enters the world of London theatre.
- Author of between 36 and 40 plays.
- 1599: the Globe Theatre built in Southwark.
- 1609: Shakespeare's sonnets published.
- 1613: the Globe Theatre burns down.
- 23rd April 1616: Shakespeare dies.
- 1623: publication of the first folio of Shakespeare's collected works.

The greatest writer ever

William Shakespeare (1564–1616) was the greatest writer who ever lived. This bold claim would meet almost no opposition in the English-speaking world and very little in the non-English-speaking world. He was a **peerless** playwright, poet and storyteller who raised the language to new heights. Hundreds of the words and phrases he coined are still used today. His work reflects as deep an understanding of the human condition as can be found in literature.

Shakespeare's early life

Remarkably little is known about Shakespeare's life. We can only be truly certain about a handful of facts, including that he was born in Stratford-upon-Avon, fathered a family there, went to London, became an actor and writer, returned to Stratford, made a will and died. While this is something of an exaggeration, there is great uncertainty over some of the most basic details, such as how many plays he wrote (somewhere between 36 and 40) and the order in which he wrote them. We have no written description of him from his own lifetime and there are doubts about the authenticity of the only portrait that may have been painted from life. Although he left nearly a million words of text, we have just 14 words in his own handwriting – his name signed six times (spelt six different ways and never as *William Shakespeare*) and the words *by me* on his will.

His life in London

In many ways, the mystery surrounding Shakespeare's life is not really important. What matters is his work. In the late 1580s or early 1590s, Shakespeare entered the thriving world of London theatre. He joined a number of theatre companies as an actor and playwright. In 1594, he became a significant shareholder in the Lord Chamberlain's Men, which had its own playhouse called the Theatre, in Shoreditch, London. The Lord Chamberlain's Men became London's leading company, frequently entertaining Queen Elizabeth I's court, and performing almost all of the most significant plays of the time. For almost two decades Shakespeare wrote two plays a year, on average.

The Globe Theatre

In 1599, the Lord Chamberlain's Men **dismantled** its theatre building and reassembled it on the south bank of the Thames in Southwark, renaming it the Globe Theatre. Shakespeare wrote his greatest plays during the first decade of its existence. His fame was established by a succession of great tragedies: *Julius Caesar, Hamlet, Othello, King Lear, Macbeth, Antony and Cleopatra* and *Coriolanus.* These tales of flawed heroes and their downfall had – and continue to have – a deep psychological appeal.

Shakespeare's historical dramas

Shakespeare's abilities as a historian have probably influenced perceptions of late medieval Britain more than any other scholar – though he was sometimes rather vague on details. The chronological span of Shakespeare's ten historical dramas runs from King John (who ruled from 1199 to 1216) to Henry VIII (who ruled from 1509 to 1547). However, they are mostly concentrated on the period between 1389 and 1485, from Richard II's personal rule to the death of Richard III. This is the era of the Hundred Years' War and the Wars of the Roses. The main subject of these dramas is the monarchy, while the **chief protagonists** come from England and France. Several of the set speeches from the history plays – 'This royal throne of kings …' (*Richard II*), 'Once more unto the breach, dear friends …' (*Henry V*), or 'Now is the winter of our discontent …' (*Richard III*) – are on a par with the great **soliloquies** of *Hamlet* or *King Lear.*

Shakespeare's later career

Shakespeare's later plays such as *Cymbeline, The Winter's Tale* and *The Tempest* are romances reflecting the growing interest in spectacle, magic and unlikely outcomes. Towards the end of his career, Shakespeare began to collaborate more with other playwrights, which suggests that his own creativity had dulled. Soon after the Globe Theatre burnt down in 1613, Shakespeare seems to have returned to Stratford, where he spent his final years.

Shakespeare's sonnets

Shakespeare was much honoured by his contemporaries – both as a poet and as a playwright. His **sonnets**, published in 1609, fall into two groups: the first 126 are addressed to a man (Mr W. H.); the remaining 28 are addressed to a woman (the 'Dark Lady'). There are many theories about who these two people may have been. As so often with Shakespeare, there is no definitive answer. But judging the quality of these poems is more straightforward. The 20th-century poet W. H. Auden claimed that the finest of the sonnets alone would have assured Shakespeare literary immortality. That remains a widely held view.

A legacy of brilliance

Shakespeare was a genius who could extract eternal truths about humankind and the nature of existence from his everyday experiences. The brilliance of his work was more the product of wisdom than knowledge. As a modern-day playwright has remarked, we badly abuse Shakespeare if we pretend he knows all the answers. He doesn't. He knows the questions.

Glossary

peerless	better than anyone or anything else
dismantled	took apart
chief protagonists	main characters
soliloquies	speeches made by a character when they are 'thinking aloud'
sonnet	14-line poem with regular rhymes

C Check your facts!

1 'Shakespeare is very highly regarded in England but not nearly so much throughout the world.' True or false?

2 What do we **not** know for certain about Shakespeare?
a) where he was born
b) how many plays he wrote
c) what he did in London
d) where he died

3 Shakespeare worked in London as a:
a) shareholder.
b) writer.
c) actor.
d) writer and actor.

4 What kind of play is *Othello*?

5 Which period do Shakespeare's historical dramas cover?
a) 1199–1547
b) 1199–1216
c) 1509–1547
d) 1389–1485

6 According to the author, why did Shakespeare begin to work more with other authors?

7 Shakespeare's sonnets were written to:
a) Mr W. H.
b) the Dark Lady.
c) W. H. Auden.
d) both Mr W. H. and the Dark Lady.

8 'The author thinks Shakespeare lived in his imagination so much that he didn't notice what was going on around him.' True or false?

D What do you think?

1 'Shakespeare fathered a family but he didn't raise one.' Explain in your own words what you understand this to mean.

2 What common themes link Shakespeare's:
a) tragedies?
b) histories?

3 'Shakespeare had a perfect knowledge of history.' True or false? Explain your answer.

4 Is Shakespeare best known for his plays or his sonnets? Explain your answer.

5 Shakespeare 'left nearly a million words of text'. Choose the best interpretation of this statement.
a) That is the actual number of words that Shakespeare wrote.
b) That is the number of Shakespeare's words that remain today.

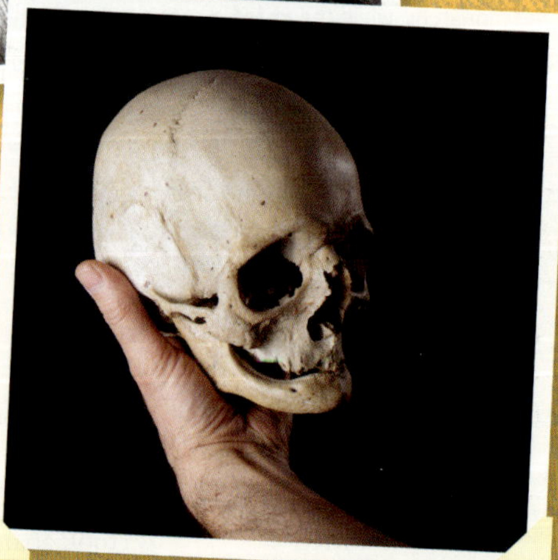

Section 2: *Topic development*

A The Seven Ages of Man

One of Shakespeare's most famous soliloquies appears in the comedy *As You Like It*. In it, a character known as 'the melancholy Jaques' reflects that the world is a stage and that people are just players (actors) who act on it. He thinks that their lives can be divided into seven acts, or ages:

All the world's a stage,
And all the men and women merely players;
They have their exits and their entrances;
And one man in his time plays many parts,
His acts being seven ages.

1 Match 1–7 to a)–g) to complete the soliloquy.

1 At first	a) the lover, sighing like furnace ...
2 Then	b) with spectacles on nose ... his big manly voice, turning again toward childish treble ...
3 And then	c) second childishness and mere oblivion
4 Then	d) a soldier, full of strange oaths ... sudden and quick in quarrel ...
5 And then	e) the justice, in fair round belly ... with eyes severe and beard of formal cut ...
6 The sixth age	f) the infant ... in the nurse's arms
7 Last scene of all is	g) the whining school-boy, with his satchel and shining morning face, creeping like snail unwillingly to school

2 Do you think Shakespeare's description of the seven ages of man is accurate?

3 Discuss the following:
- Which age of man are you at now?
- Is it a good age? Why/why not?
- Are you looking forward to the next age of man?
- Do you miss an age you have left behind? Why/why not?

B Shakespeare in everyday English

1 English-speakers today use many phrases coined (made up) by Shakespeare, often without knowing it. Work with a partner to match the Shakespearean phrases on the left with their meanings on the right. Use a dictionary if you get stuck.

what the dickens?	it makes no sense at all
beggars all description	the time when you are young and innocent
a foregone conclusion	our past
in my mind's eye	a person who gives great support to others
it's Greek to me	what can that be?
salad days	something that is certain to happen
love is blind	in my visual imagination
play fast and loose	cannot possibly be described
a tower of strength	people in love don't know what they are doing
all our yesterdays	behave irresponsibly, without morals

2 Now put the right idiom in each of the following five sentences.

a) I don't know ____ ___ ______ he's trying to do!

b) The result between Manchester United and Barnet in the FA Cup is _ ________ ________; Barnet don't stand a chance.

c) In my ____ ___ I was very idealistic and always thought the best of everyone.

d) David has been _ ____ __ ______ for us over this difficult period.

e) I wouldn't like to work with them – in my opinion, they ____ ____ ___ _____ with the rules.

3 After checking the answers with your teacher, work with a partner to write five sentences illustrating the other idioms. Read them to another pair but without saying the idiom. See if they can guess which idiom should go in your sentence.

Section 3: *Extension activities*

A Discuss

There is still some doubt about the true identity of Shakespeare. Discuss how/if our view of his work would change if it was discovered that Shakespeare was:

- a woman.
- more than one person.
- from another country.
- Scottish.
- a murderer.
- a prince.

B Research

Search for: 'Globe Theatre' / 'Kiss Me Kate' + 'West Side Story' / 'Shakespeare' + 'the Scottish play'

1 Find out about the modern Globe Theatre in London.
- Where exactly is it?
- Who founded it?
- Which plays does it put on?

2 Find out which two Shakespeare plays were the basis for the famous American musicals *Kiss Me Kate* and *West Side Story*.
- Who wrote the music for each?
- Who starred in the original productions?
- When were they made?
- What are the most famous songs in them?
- Which song actually mentions Shakespeare?

3 Find out about the theatrical superstition relating to Shakespeare's 'Scottish play'.
- Which play is it?
- What is the superstition?
- What is the origin of the superstition?
- What can you do to prevent evil if someone mentions it in a theatre?
- Do you think there is any truth in it? Why/why not?

C Write

Read this famous sonnet by Shakespeare about true love. Don't worry if you can't understand it all – many native English speakers would have the same problem. Pay attention to the rhythm and rhyme of the sonnet.

Sonnet 116

Let me not to the marriage of true minds
Admit impediments; love is not love
Which alters when it alteration finds,
Or bends with the remover to remove.
O no, it is an ever-fixed mark
That looks on tempests and is never shaken;
It is the star to every wandering bark,
Whose worth's unknown, although his height be taken.
Love's not Time's fool, though rosy lips and cheeks
Within his bending sickle's compass come;
Love alters not with his brief hours and weeks,
But bears it out even to the edge of doom.
If this be error and upon me proved,
I never writ, nor no man ever loved.

Write a sonnet. It should have 14 lines, about 10 syllables per line, and some of it should rhyme. It can be about anything you like. (100 words)

15 The sun never set:
The British Empire

Section 1: *Reading*

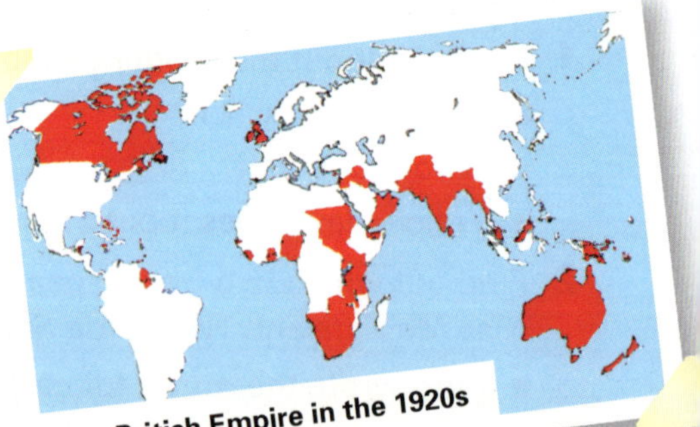

The British Empire in the 1920s

A Before you read – think and discuss

Britain is a small island located at the edge of Europe. It once ruled over the largest empire the world has ever seen.

- Has your country ever had an empire or been a colony?
- Are all empires the same? Are they usually a force for good or bad?
- What, if anything, do you know about the British Empire?

B Read the text

The sun never set:
The British Empire

'We seem ... to have conquered and peopled half the world in a fit of absence of mind.'

Sir John Seeley (English essayist and historian, writing in 1883)

At a glance

Dates: from late 16th century to mid-20th century

Area: covered a quarter of the world's land area – approx. 14 million square miles

Locations: colonies were established in India, the Caribbean, North America, the Pacific and South East Asia (including Singapore and Hong Kong), Australasia, the Middle East and parts of Africa (including Egypt, Sudan and Zimbabwe)

Population: by 1922 a fifth of the world's population (about 500 million people) belonged to the British Empire

Decline: in the 20th century, particularly after the Second World War

Two sides of empire

The debate about the British Empire is one of the most controversial in British history. There are two strongly opposing views. One sees the empire as a dreadful story of enslavement, **exploitation**, theft, greed, cruelty and massacre. The other sees it as a tale of enormous energy and enterprise, of idealistic people who really did believe they were making the world a better place and helping those less fortunate than themselves.

Origins and development of the British Empire

At its peak, in around 1920, the British Empire was the biggest ever known. It covered a quarter of the world's land area – some 14 million square miles – and a fifth of its population, about 500 million people. Although much of the land was added in the 19th century, the British Empire began **in earnest** during the Tudor age with the settlement of Virginia in 1585. It grew out of the great seafaring voyages of that era, and in its first 300 years it was a loose arrangement of trading posts defended by the Royal Navy and run by private companies whose job it was to administer colonies and oversee trade. The best known was the East India Company, founded in 1599.

The 'first' British Empire

The first Indian colony was established in 1610 and the first Caribbean one in 1623. The Empire expanded steadily thereafter, partly through the growth of British trade, and partly as a result of wars with other colonial powers, especially France and Spain.

The Seven Years' War (1756–63), for example, saw Britain take control of much of India and Canada. That marked the peak of what later came to be called the 'first' British Empire. The rebellion of the 13 American colonies, originally against Britain's trading restrictions, brought it to an end in 1776.

The 'second' British Empire

But even while America was being lost, Captain Cook was exploring new imperial possibilities in the Antipodes. The first colony there, New South Wales, was set up in 1788. Sierra Leone in west Africa was established as a home for freed slaves at around the same time. By the middle of the 19th century, Britain held possessions in every **habitable** continent, giving rise to the boast that 'the sun never set' on the British Empire. Somewhere, in a British-held territory, it was daylight.

The growth of imperialism

The prime minister Disraeli made Queen Victoria Empress of India in 1877. By the 1880s, the British had developed a conscious mood of **imperialism**. Britain now made concerted efforts to grow its empire. Under the government of the supposedly anti-imperialist prime minister W. E. Gladstone, Britain took control of Egypt in 1882. This sparked off the so-called 'scramble for Africa', which added much of the eastern and southern part of the continent to Britain's collection. The **ideology** of imperialism was partly based on a '**social Darwinist**' belief in the racial superiority of white people. But there was also a more liberal view which saw the imperial mission as **benign**. The Empire was designed not to exploit people but to free them from poverty, ignorance and superstition.

20th-century additions

The only substantial additions to the British Empire in the 20th century were the 'mandated' territories – ex-German and Ottoman possessions, including much of the Middle East – allocated to it after the First World War. They were not meant to be 'colonies', though most people at the time regarded them as such.

The decline of the British Empire

The Second World War saw the start of imperial decline. Approximately 5 million people from 50 different nationalities fought in the British armed services during the war. Three and a half million of these were non-white people who chose to fight fascism despite nationalist pressure at home to revolt against the British. But paradoxically, this tended to strengthen the national self-confidence of colonial people rather than their loyalty to Britain. Then, after 1945, the huge financial cost of defeating Germany, coupled with the burden of the Cold War against the Soviet Union, made it harder for the British to maintain their empire. As a result of these pressures, India, for so long the 'jewel in the crown' of the empire, was partitioned and, together with Pakistan, granted independence in 1947. Palestine was handed over to the United Nations in the same year.

A wind of change

Britain's **ever-diminishing** world role after 1945 was confirmed by prime minister Harold Macmillan in March 1960 when he **heralded** 'a wind of change' blowing across Africa. A rapid process of decolonization got under way soon after. Sixty-four nations saw the end of British rule between the independence of India in 1947 and the ceding of Hong Kong to China in 1997. The once vast, **sprawling** empire had all but disappeared by 1980 with the creation of Zimbabwe.

One leading historian of the empire has recently coined the phrase 'Anglobalization' to describe how for centuries Britain exercised its power through its imperial possessions. The British Empire gave capitalism, parliamentary democracy, the English language, railway travel, cricket and football to the world. This was quite an achievement. However, in the process, millions of people were enslaved and exploited. The writer Rudyard Kipling famously called empire-building 'the white man's burden'. But even at its kindest, the main economic beneficiaries of empire were always the British. The burden was, in reality, carried by the colonized and not the colonizer.

Glossary

exploitation	using for your own benefit
in earnest	in a serious way
habitable	possible to live in
imperialism	policy of extending a country's power and influence through colonization
ideology	belief system
social Darwinist	the idea that people are affected by the same laws of natural selection as plants and animals
benign	gentle and kind
ever-diminishing	getting smaller all the time
heralded	marked the arrival of
sprawling	spread out irregularly over a large area

C Check your facts!

1 'Everyone now agrees the British Empire was a force for good.' True or false?

2 Where and when did the British Empire really start?

3 The 'first' British Empire did not have colonies in:
a) America.
b) France and Spain.
c) India.
d) the Caribbean.

4 'Britain even had colonies in Antarctica.' True or false?

5 British imperialism was:
a) a social Darwinist ideology.
b) a liberal ideology.
c) a combination of liberal and social Darwinist ideology.
d) not an ideology.

6 The First World War left the British Empire:
a) bigger.
b) smaller.
c) the same size as before the war.

7 The 'jewel in the crown' of the British Empire was:
a) India.
b) Pakistan.
c) Palestine.
d) Britain itself.

8 'Britain had no colonies left by 1980.' True or false?

9 Which two sports did the British Empire give to the world?

D What do you think?

1 Was it more true of the first or second British Empire that it was acquired in a 'fit of absence of mind'? Give reasons for your answer.

2 'The sun never sets on the British Empire.' What did this expression mean in its:
a) literal sense?
b) non-literal sense?

3 How did the impact of the Second World War on the British Empire differ from that of the First World War? Give specific details.

4 The 'wind of change' referred to:
a) climate change in Africa.
b) the end of British rule in India.
c) the election of Harold Macmillan.
d) political change in Africa.

5 Do you think the author considers the British Empire was more of a good thing or a bad thing? Give your reasons.

Section 2: *Topic development*

A Slavery

Though Britain itself never had many slaves, the 'first' British Empire grew rich on the transatlantic slave trade. Read the account below of how this worked, filling in gaps with the **sequencing** and **contrast** words in the box. Check your answers with a partner.

Sequencing words	Contrast words
previously Ultimately finally Then following When eventually Meanwhile First After during Next next	Despite though However

1. a) ________, a British trader bought a ship. b) ________ they loaded it with British products that were in demand in Africa – guns and gunpowder, beads, copper kettles, cloth, nails and pans.
2. a) ________ they sailed to West Africa. b) ________ arriving, they unloaded the ship and traded the products for black African slaves. These people had c) ________ been either bought or captured by slave traders based in Africa. Most of the traders were white Europeans. d) ________, black Africans were also involved in the capture and sale of people from other tribes.
3. The a) ________ stage of the journey was the crossing to America and the Caribbean, b) ________ which many slaves died because of the terrible conditions on board. c) ________ this, it was still a very profitable business.
4. a) ________ they b) ________ reached the other side of the Atlantic, they swapped the slaves for sugar, cotton, tobacco and rum.
5. The ship a) ________ returned home and sold these valuable commodities for a high profit.
6. a) ________, the slaves were put to work by their new owners in the sugar, cotton and tobacco plantations of America and the Caribbean.
7. An estimated 11 million Africans were transported in this way. a) ________, this terrible human traffic was stopped by the British Empire and its navy, even b) ________ Britain had got very rich from the slave trade.

B William Wilberforce and the abolition of slavery

Economic development and the resistance of the slaves themselves were key factors in bringing about the end of slavery. But the roles of the anti-slavery campaigner William Wilberforce and the Royal Navy were also vital in ending the trade itself.

1 Read this account of Wilberforce's role, choosing the correct tense alternative for each verb.

William Wilberforce ***was / had been born*** on 24th August 1759 in Hull and ***became / had become*** MP for that city in 1780. But the most important date in his life is probably 1785, when he had a conversion to evangelical Christianity. From that date on, he ***dedicated / had dedicated*** his life and work to the service of God. He ***was / had been*** a dissolute young man at Cambridge University, playing cards, drinking and gambling late into the night. This lifestyle ***continued / had continued*** when he became an MP. He ***was / had been*** popular socially and an eloquent speaker in Parliament.

Wilberforce's main aim following his conversion ***was / had been*** to promote Christian values in public and private life. In 1783 he ***heard / had heard*** first-hand accounts of the terrible conditions on slave ships and Caribbean plantations, but it ***was not / had not been*** until 1787 that he ***became / had become*** actively involved in a campaign to end the slave trade. Another Cambridge graduate, Thomas Clarkson, ***was / had been*** a huge influence on him. Clarkson and his fellow 'abolitionists' ***were / had been*** campaigning for an end to the slave trade – they ***thought / had thought*** it was unchristian, and ***were / had been*** horrified by the greed of the slave owners and traders. Clarkson ***brought / had brought*** Wilberforce a copy of a book he had published calling for an end to slavery, and also first-hand evidence about the slave trade. Others, including the prime minister William Pitt, ***encouraged / had encouraged*** Wilberforce to act on his beliefs.

Wilberforce ***sensed / had sensed*** a call from God, writing in a journal entry in 1787 that 'God Almighty ***set / had set*** before me two great objects, the suppression of the Slave Trade and the Reformation of Manners [morals]'.

For 18 years, Wilberforce ***introduced / had introduced*** anti-slavery motions in Parliament. He ***was / had been*** supported by a range of abolitionists who ***opposed / had opposed*** slavery usually for religious reasons. They ***raised / had raised*** public awareness of their cause with pamphlets, books, rallies and petitions. The Slave Trade Act finally ***became / had become*** law on 25th March 1807, making it illegal to carry men in British ships to be sold as slaves. Wilberforce's face ***streamed / had been streaming*** with tears. It ***was / had not been***, however, not until 1833 that an act ***was / had been*** passed giving freedom to all slaves in the British Empire. Wilberforce ***died / had died*** the previous month.

2 Check your answers with a partner, then in class.

3 Now go through the passage together and name each of the tenses used.

4 Discuss what the rules are about when to use each one.

Section 3: *Extension activities*

A Discuss

Study the two quotes below, then discuss the questions that follow.

'Remember that you are an Englishman, and have consequently won first prize in the lottery of life.' Cecil Rhodes, 19th-century English imperialist

'I know why the sun never sets on the British Empire; God wouldn't trust an Englishman in the dark.' J. Duncan Speith, American writer

1 What do you think the two speakers are really saying in these quotes?

2 Which one do you prefer? Why?

3 Which one do you think is closer to the truth? Why?

B Research

Search for: 'the Commonwealth' / 'Kipling' + 'white man's burden' + 'Disney' / 'slave trade' + 'apology' + 'Church of England' + 'Mayor of London' + 'British government'

1 Find out about the Commonwealth.
- What is its connection with the British Empire?
- How many countries are members?
- What does it do?
- Who is its figurehead?

2 Find out about Rudyard Kipling and the 'white man's burden'.
- Which country did he want to 'take up the white man's burden'?
- Which part of the world had it just colonized?
- How did he view colonized people in the poem?
- Which famous Disney cartoon was based on a Kipling story?

3 Find out if the following have apologized for the slave trade.
- the British government
- the Church of England
- the Mayor of London

C Write

Do you think the British Empire was more of a force for good or for evil?

Think about:
- beneficiaries
- victims
- positive aspects – football, the English language
- negative aspects – slavery, exploitation
- other empires
- former colonies today

(250 words)

16 A special relationship? Britain and the USA

Section 1: *Reading*

A Before you read – think and discuss

The USA was born out of revolt against Britain and has far outgrown its former colonial master. Yet many believe that the two countries still have a 'special relationship'.

- Does your country have a 'special relationship' with any other country?
- What are such relationships based on?
- How important do you think language is in bringing countries together?
- What, if anything, do you know about the relationship between Britain and the USA since American independence?

B Read the text

A special relationship?

Britain and the USA

'England and America are two countries divided by a common language.' George Bernard Shaw

To the generation of Britons who lived through the Second World War, the Atlantic Ocean seemed narrower than the English Channel. Europe was geographically close, but the British viewed their neighbours with suspicion. By contrast, the 3,000 or so miles between Britain and the USA were easily bridged by the bonds of history, culture and language.

Britain's longing for American friendship has influenced its diplomacy for nearly a century. Yet it was once very different. America was part of the British Empire until 1776, when 13 British colonies rose up against the 'mother country'. Under George Washington, their Continental Army defeated the forces of King George III, leading to the birth of what would become the richest and most powerful country in history.

Thriving trade helped the British and their ex-colonists to coexist. This was briefly interrupted by the **inconclusive** War of 1812, during which British forces burned down the White House. Although this was the last military conflict between the two nations, they nearly went to war again over Venezuela in 1895. Consequently, by the start of the 20th century Britain and the USA were more rivals than friends and certainly did not see themselves as part of a greater English-speaking entity.

When the First World War erupted in Europe in 1914, US President Woodrow Wilson was determined that it would not become America's war. 'The United States must,' he insisted, 'be neutral in fact as well as in name.' In the end, however, repeated attacks on American ships by German U-boats forced him into action. America's military contribution to the Western Front from April 1917 to November 1918 helped to bring about the Allied victory. And after the war, it became clear that the USA's huge economic strength had tipped the balance of power its way.

The outbreak of the Second World War in 1939 was an unpleasant reminder to Americans that European states could disrupt the trade on which their wealth depended. This time round, the country played a different role. It did not stay strictly neutral. Under the 1941 Lend-Lease Act, it supplied

Britain with food and weapons on credit, which Britain did not have to pay back until after the war. This gave a huge boost to the country's war effort. Prime Minister Churchill called it the 'most unselfish and **unsordid** financial act of any country in all history.' But what Churchill longed for most of all was direct US military intervention. In his attempts to woo the Americans, he made much of the alleged 'special relationship' between the two nations (indeed it was he who first used the term). His own mother, he often reminded them, was American.

In the event, America entered the Second World War **in retaliation for** the Japanese bombing of Pearl Harbor in December 1941. Nearly two million American soldiers arrived in Britain before the Allied invasion of Nazi-occupied Europe (the 1944 D-Day landings). The relationship between the American soldiers and their hosts wasn't always smooth. A popular saying of the time was that these soldiers (also known as GIs) were 'overpaid, overfed, oversexed and over here'. Young British males were envious of the GIs, mainly for their supposed success with British women, apparently helped by the GIs' supplies of chewing gum and nylon stockings. A mass survey in 1943 found that only one-third of Britons approved of their saviours from 'across the pond'. But the Allies triumphed over Nazi Germany, and Churchill and President Roosevelt made a great display of unity, though some questioned how close they were. One of Churchill's advisers observed, 'the war was all they had in common'.

The Cold War against communism ensured that Anglo-American friendship outlasted the war against Hitler. The power balance, though, became even more unequal. In each decade from the 1940s to the 1980s there were moments when Britain's economic survival depended on American financial aid. International events also proved that Britain could no longer pursue a foreign policy independent of American wishes. During the Suez Crisis of 1956, intense pressure from the USA led to Britain's humiliating withdrawal from its military action in Egypt. A former US secretary of state later observed that Britain 'has lost an empire but not yet found a role in the world.'

Britain under Margaret Thatcher in the 1980s once again found that role. She made a revitalized special relationship with the USA central to it. This was eased by the personal and ideological **rapport** she shared with President Ronald Reagan. Together they voiced a certainty of mission: to bring about the downfall of world communism and the Soviet Union, which Reagan described as the 'evil empire'.

As the new century began, Anglo-American unity expressed itself in a series of joint military campaigns. Prime Minister Tony Blair (1997–2007) enthusiastically locked Britain into President Bush's 'War on Terror' in Afghanistan and Iraq. Although Britain suddenly achieved an importance on the world stage it had not had since Churchill, Blair paid a political price at home. Ordinary Britons and influential thinkers savagely criticized what they saw as London's **subservient** relationship with Washington. Britain was often referred to as being America's '51st state' rather than as an equal in a supposed 'special relationship'.

Glossary

inconclusive	without a winner
unsordid	clean, noble
in retaliation for	in revenge for
rapport	a close or sympathetic relationship
subservient	serving or acting in an obedient and inferior way

C Check your facts!

1 Which of the following were the bonds between Britain and the USA **not** based on?
a) history
b) geography
c) language
d) culture

2 Who was on the throne of Britain when the country lost its American colonies?

3 'The Venezuelan crisis of 1895 was the last military conflict between Britain and the USA.' True or false?

4 The USA was involved in the First World War:
a) for under a year.
b) for over a year.
c) at no point in the conflict.
d) from the start.

5 'The Lend-Lease Act meant that the USA was not strictly neutral in the Second World War.' True or false?

6 How many American soldiers came to Britain during the Second World War?

7 The 1956 Suez Crisis showed that Britain:
a) was still the USA's strongest ally.
b) now had to do what the USA wanted.
c) still had an important role in the world.
d) was as strong and independent as ever.

8 Who did Ronald Reagan mean when he spoke about 'the evil empire'?

9 'Tony Blair's involvement in the "War on Terror" increased his unpopularity at home.' True or false? Give reasons.

D What do you think?

1 Explain what you think the author means by 'a greater English-speaking entity'.

2 'The USA joined both world wars as a result of attacks by hostile powers rather than out of a desire to help Britain.' True or false? Give reasons.

3 Explain the play on words in the Second World War saying about the American soldiers being 'overpaid, overfed, oversexed and over here'.

4 According to the text, who got on best?
a) George III and George Washington
b) Churchill and Roosevelt
c) Thatcher and Reagan
d) Blair and Bush

5 Britain and the USA have both helped each other at different times in history. Identify which country has given the other help that is:
a) only military.
b) both military and financial.

Section 2: *Topic development*

A Common language?

Most people know that American English has a different accent from British English. But there are also differences in everyday words, such as *trunk* and *boot*, *lift* and *elevator*, *nappy* and *diaper*.

1 Match these educational terms, which often cause confusion.

primary school	college student
secondary school	private school
public school	major
university student	elementary school
lecturer	high school
main subject	professor

2 Which are the British terms and which the American?

3 Tell your partner about your education, using the British English terms for these things.

B Noah Webster: revolutionary speller

1 Read this short account of the work of the great American lexicographer, Noah Webster, filling in the blanks with the words in the box.

replaced	aristocracy	edition	dictionaries	famous	usage	Father

Noah Webster (1758 –1843) has been called the a) '__________ of American Scholarship and Education'. He believed that the English b) __________ had corrupted English spelling and grammar with their old-fashioned rules and obsession with Greek and Latin grammar. American English, he felt, should be based on 'republican principles' and follow popular c) __________.

With his spellers and d) __________, he slowly changed American English spelling. He e) __________ *c* with *s* in words like *defense,* changed the *re* to *er* in words like *center,* dropped one of the *l*s in *traveler* and similar words, and eventually dropped the *u* in words like *colour* or *favour*. He also got rid of most *ough* spellings and many other silent letters.

Webster published his f) __________ *American Dictionary of the English Language* in 1828, at the age of 70. Of its 70,000 words, 12,000 had never appeared in a dictionary before. He died in 1843, not long after completing the second g) __________, though his work was still largely unrecognized.

2 Now work with a partner to identify which words in the box below are spelt the American way and which the British.

catalogue dialog doughnut favorite humour counselor
(a) license metre omelette program

Write down how you think each is spelt in the other version of English.

3 Discuss in groups.

- Which spelling system do you prefer? Give reasons.
- Do you think one country should adopt the other's system? How easy would this be?
- Has your country ever tried to change its spelling rules? What happened?

C A misunderestimated man?

Whether or not he had a special relationship with Britain, President George W. Bush certainly had an interesting relationship with the English language. A lot of people made fun of his use of it.

1 Study the following famous 'Bushisms' with a partner, then try to translate them into good, clear English.

They misunderestimated me.

I think when the history of this period is written, people will realize a lot of the decisions that were made ... took place over a decade or so, before I arrived in President, during I arrived in President.

Families is where our nation finds hope, where wings take dream.

I know how hard it is for you to put food on your family.

Rarely is the questioned asked: is our children learning?

2 Discuss how important you think it is for a leader to use language well. Are there good leaders who use language badly and bad leaders who use language well? Give examples if possible.

Section 3: *Extension activities*

A Discuss

When the Founding Fathers were writing the Constitution of the USA (1787), there was some doubt about what the new country's official language would be. The main competitors were German and English. Would history have been different if they had chosen German? Think about:

- the First and Second World Wars.
- the 'special relationship' with Britain.
- Hollywood films.
- jazz, rock and roll, pop, hip-hop, rap.
- the Internet.

B Research

Search for: 'George W. Bush' + 'Churchill' / 'H. L. Mencken' + 'the American language' / 'verbing' + 'America'

1 Find out about what George W. Bush thought of Winston Churchill.
- Did he admire him?
- Did he try to follow Churchill's example in any way?
- Does this tell you anything about the 'special relationship'? If so, what?
- Do you think Churchill would have approved of Bush? Why/why not?

2 Find out about H. L. Mencken and his work on 'the American language'.
- Who was Mencken?
- What was his view of the American language?
- How many volumes did he write on the American language?
- Did people take him seriously as a scholar?

3 Find out about the linguistic habit of 'verbing', which is perhaps most common in American English.
- What exactly is it?
- Give some examples.
- Do you think these words are improved by being turned into verbs? Give reasons.
- Suggest some other words that could be verbed.
- What do you think their enthusiasm for verbing tells us about Americans?

C Write

Do you prefer British or American English? Answer this question, giving your reasons. Write about:

- accent and the sound of the language.
- spelling.
- usefulness.
- associations of the language.
- culture – films, books, comics, etc.
- education.
- whether we can say one kind of English is 'better' than another. (250 words)

17 A funny old game: Cricket

Section 1: *Reading*

A Before you read – think and discuss

Cricket is England's national summer sport, and many people think its sportsmanship and sense of fair play reflect the English national character.

- What is your country's national sport?
- What other sports are popular?
- What other sports are popular in the UK?
- What, if anything, do you know about the sport of cricket?

B Read the text

A FUNNY OLD GAME

'[Cricket is] more than a game. It's an institution.' *Author Thomas Hughes in* **Tom Brown's Schooldays**

The summer game of cricket has an extremely long history and can be traced back to the 13th century. It is perhaps the most English (though not British) of all organized sports and certainly holds a deep cultural significance for the English. The game is a symbol of fair play and the love of tradition; for instance, the phrase 'it's not cricket' is used to express disapproval of any kind of **misconduct**. Its status beyond being simply a game is also reflected by the fact that cricket does not have *rules* but *laws*.

The world's leading cricketing nations, apart from England, are Australia, India, New Zealand, Pakistan, Sri Lanka, South Africa and the West Indies. Cricket was introduced into all these countries during the era of the British Empire.

Cricket has its **detractors**. Non-followers of the game mistakenly view cricket as a **toffs**' game that appeals only to the wealthy and privileged. These criticisms might appear to have some merit. Until 1962, a clear distinction was drawn between amateur players, known as *Gentlemen*, and professionals, known as *Players*. There was something very English, not to say ridiculous, about the class snobbery of this. Gentlemen's initials were traditionally written on scorecards before the surname; the Players' initials were written after it, because it was believed they should be addressed by their surname only. In 1961, in a match played at Lord's Cricket Ground in London, the so-called home of cricket, the following correction was read out to the crowd: 'Your cards show, at Number 8 for Middlesex, F. J. Titmus. We have to apologize for this mistake. That should read, of course, Titmus F. J.' Yet despite such examples of snobbery, cricket has traditionally been played by millions of ordinary English children in schools and parks over the summer months.

Cricket is also accused of being boring. The most **prestigious** version of the sport, international Test Match cricket, is played over a period of up to five days (six hours per day minimum). For all that, many Test Matches still result in a draw. A foreign observer once remarked that the English, since they lacked any spiritual instinct, had invented cricket in order to give themselves a sense of eternity.

The most famous of all English cricketers is the extraordinary, larger-than-life W. G. Grace, a Bristol doctor whose cricket career spanned the period from 1865 to 1908. Cricket is an individual game played within a team context, and as a consequence statistics are used extensively to judge players' achievements. Most players are either batsmen or bowlers, but Grace was a brilliant all-rounder, setting records for both batting and bowling. He was the first-ever cricketer to do the 'double' – scoring 1,000 runs and taking 100 wickets in one season. Perhaps understandably, Grace had a very high opinion of his own talents. He once went in to bat for Gloucestershire, his county team, in front of a large and expectant crowd. Having scored only a handful of runs, Grace was given out by the **umpire** but refused to leave the field and instructed the official to change his decision. 'The crowd has come to see me bat,' Grace explained calmly, 'not you umpire.' This was definitely 'not cricket'!

W. G. Grace

The most significant international **rivalry** in cricket, that between England and Australia, would have been familiar to W. G. Grace, who played in many Test Matches for England against Australia. The two countries played their first Test Match against each other in Melbourne, Australia, in March 1877. Much to the surprise and horror of the English, the match ended in a victory for Australia, as did a Test Match they played five years later at the Kennington Oval, London, in August 1882. For some, the shock of being beaten at home was too much to bear. On the following day, the *Sporting Times* newspaper published a mock **obituary** for English cricket (see below). The following winter (1882–83), the English team went to Australia and won two of the three Test Matches played. At the end of the third match, some Australian women burnt the ball or part of the wicket (no one knows for certain which) and presented the ashes to the English captain. And so was born the concept of the Ashes, which the two countries continue to contest to this day.

In Affectionate Remembrance
of
ENGLISH CRICKET,
Which Died at the Oval on
29th AUGUST, 1882,
Deeply Lamented by a Large Circle of Sorrowing Friends and Acquaintances.
R.I.P.
N.B.—The Body will be Cremated and the Ashes taken to Australia.

Glossary

misconduct	bad behaviour
detractors	people who are critical of someone or something
toffs	informal and disrespectful term for members of the upper class
prestigious	respected, admired
umpire	referee
rivalry	competition for the same outcome
obituary	an article in a newspaper about someone who has died
R.I.P.	rest in peace
cremated	when the remains, usually of a dead person's body, have been burnt to ashes

C Check your facts!

1 How old is cricket?

2 What was the main factor in spreading cricket all over the world?
a) modern communications
b) the English language
c) the British Empire
d) the fans' enthusiasm

3 'Cricket is just a game for the upper classes.' True or false?

4 'The fact that Test Matches last for days means that you always get a clear winner.' True or false?

5 An 'all-rounder' in cricket is:
a) good at both batting and bowling.
b) overweight and larger-than-life.
c) better at batting than bowling.
d) better at bowling than batting.

6 Where was the first Test Match between England and Australia played?

D What do you think?

1 The author thinks cricket is a 'funny old game'. Do you think he/she means funny ha-ha! (comical) or funny peculiar (strange)? Explain your answer.

2 'It's clear from the text that the Scots and Irish love cricket as much as the English.' True or false?

3 Explain in your own words what the three expressions below mean.
a) fair play
b) class snobbery
c) larger-than-life

4 Which of these answers is **not** correct? The foreign observer who said the English had invented cricket to give themselves a sense of eternity meant:
a) cricket matches seemed to go on forever.
b) the English were not very spiritual.
c) only religious people were good at cricket.
d) cricket was a sort of substitute for religion.

Section 2: *Topic development*

A Cricket idioms*

***idiom:** a special set phrase whose meaning is not always clear from the individual words in it

1 Cricket has been a central feature of English life for centuries and because of this is the source of many idioms in the language.

Match the cricket expressions a)–e) with their literal meanings i)–v). Use a dictionary to help you if necessary.

a) to be stumped	___	i) a cricket pitch after rain, difficult to bat on
b) to hit/knock for six	___	ii) to bowl a tricky and unpredictable ball
c) a sticky wicket	___	iii) to be got out by the gloved catcher behind the wicket
d) a straight bat	___	iv) to score maximum runs by hitting the ball over the boundary without it touching the ground
e) to bowl a googly	___	v) the classic defensive batting position, with the bat parallel to your legs

2 Study the same cricket expressions used as idioms. Choose the best meaning for the cricket idioms. Circle i, ii or iii.

a) The announcement **knocked her for six**; she had to sit down and think about what this meant for her.
i) to make someone feel young ii) to make someone feel very shocked
iii) to physically attack someone

b) It was all going very well until they **bowled a googly** and demanded to know when I had stopped telling the truth.
i) to tell a lie ii) to ask someone something unexpected and difficult to answer
iii) to be careful and efficient

c) He's **on a very sticky wicket** and might get in serious trouble if he's not careful.
i) to be in a difficult situation ii) to be unsteady on your feet
iii) to be immoral and devious

d) I'd recommend **keeping a very straight bat** at the interview – don't try any clever answers.
i) to be confident ii) to talk loudly iii) to be honest and straightforward

e) When they asked him that question about tax, **he was** completely **stumped** – he looked clueless and stopped talking.
i) to be very shy ii) to be argumentative and angry
iii) to be unable to explain or answer something

3 Write three sentences about your own life, using the idioms above.

I'm stumped by this exercise!
I knew I was on a sticky wicket the day I started that job.
Getting ill just before the exam knocked me for six.

4 What sporting idioms are there in your language? Explain them to a partner.

TIP! **Try to work out the meaning from the context, rather than by using a dictionary.**

B Sledging: not cricket?

1 Read the text below. Do you think 'sledging' is fair play?

Sledging is the practice of putting opponents off their game by insulting them and belittling their efforts, preferably in a witty manner. It happens all over the cricketing world, but is thought to have originated in Australia. Here are a few examples:

Bowler: *[to batsman, who cannot hit the ball]* It's red, round and weighs about five ounces.
Batsman: *[after hitting the ball out of the ground]* You know what it looks like, now go and find it.

Bowler: *[to batsman]* I've been waiting two years for another chance to humiliate you.
Batsman: Looks like you spent it eating.

Fielder: *[to batsman]* Does your husband play cricket as well?

2 In 2009, the Board for Cricket Control in India proposed a ban on sledging. What are the arguments for and against sledging? Discuss your ideas and make notes.

For	Against
a) cricket is a competitive sport; sledging puts players in a competitive mood	a) cricket is a 'gentleman's sport', and sledging is not gentlemanly
b) sledging is just harmless fun	b) cricketers should not have to resort to abuse

3 Once you have finished your discussion and made notes, have a vote on whether you think sledging should be banned.

4 Would sledging be considered acceptable at international sporting events in your country? Why/why not?

Section 3: *Extension activities*

A Discuss

The distinguished English writer George Orwell said that sport was 'war minus the shooting'. Discuss with a partner or in groups:

- what you think he meant by this.
- if you agree (give reasons).
- whether you think international sport brings people closer together or turns countries against each other (think about major sporting events such as the Olympics or the football World Cup).
- if sport and politics can ever really be separated.

B Research

Search for: 'Test Match records' + 'Wisden' / 'Basil D'Oliveira' / 'cricket as explained to a foreigner'

1 Cricket is a sport that relies heavily on statistics. Use the Internet or get a copy of *Wisden Cricketer's Almanac* from the library and find out:

- which batsman has scored the most runs in Test Match history.
- which bowler has taken the most wickets in Test Match history.
- who is considered to be the greatest Test Match cricketer of all time.

2 Use the Internet to find out as much as you can about Basil D'Oliveira and the political controversy surrounding his Test cricket career. Make notes on what this tells you about:

- sport and politics.
- racism in 1960s Britain.
- the people who managed English cricket at that time.

Be prepared to discuss your findings in class and to say how much you think Britain has changed since D'Oliveira's day.

3 Search for 'Cricket as explained to a foreigner' to find a well-known text that appears in cricket clubs, in cricket books, on cricket websites and even on tea towels for tourists.

a) Can you understand the rules as explained in this text?
b) Do you think you are meant to understand them?
c) What word would you use to describe the tone of this text?

C Write

Describe the most exciting sporting event you have ever watched or taken part in. Include:

- what happened, when and where.
- why it was so exciting and memorable.
- your feelings about it. (250 words)

18 Seen and not heard: British childhood

Section 1: *Reading*

A Before you read – think and discuss

Historically, the British have a reputation for being uncaring towards their children. By contrast, many people say modern British parents are too soft on their children.

- Is there a difference in the way that the societies of different countries treat their children?
- Was childhood the same for your parents, grandparents and great-grandparents as it was for you, or have things changed?
- What is special about childhood compared with other stages of life?
- What, if anything, do you know about British childhood now and in the past?

B Read the text

Seen and not heard: British childhood

The concept of childhood is a surprisingly recent one. Before about the 17th century, there was no special vocabulary used to distinguish children from adults. Children had no distinctive clothing or games, and in art no attempt was made to represent them as children, just as miniature adults.

The origins of British childhood date back to the 1600s, when wealthy families began to display concern for the moral development and education of children. These families viewed their children as fragile creatures of God to be nurtured and improved. Over time, this attitude passed on to middle-class families, where attention focused on the health, hygiene and education of the child. In addition, the actual length of childhood gradually extended with the expansion of the school system.

An extraordinary number of children's books, with *Tom Brown's Schooldays* by Thomas Hughes (1857) being one of the first and most famous, are set at school. The massively popular *Harry Potter* books are a modern example of this tradition. Harry, like so many fictional creations before him, goes to a **boarding school**, the sort of institution traditionally attended by the sons of the British ruling class.

Victorian wisdom was that children should be 'seen and not heard'. For many upper- and middle-class boys, the reality was that they were neither seen nor heard as their otherwise kind parents sent them away from home at an early age to boarding schools. Some historians explain this peculiarly British custom as a way of continuing the class system. Others believe that Britain's empire demanded both nurseries for children of parents in distant colonies and training grounds for the tough leaders of the future.

Rather confusingly, the British call these institutions *public* schools. During the 19th century, elite fee-paying schools such as Eton, Rugby, Harrow, Marlborough and Westminster developed a clear pattern and identity. The school chapel became the focal point of life, discipline was enforced through **prefects** and the emphasis was on team games. Dr Thomas Arnold, headmaster of Rugby from 1828 to 1842, stamped his imprint on public school education more than anyone else in this era. He believed in what has been termed 'muscular Christianity'. Arnold's weekly **sermons** were aimed at improving the character of the boys and filling them with a sense of duty to the community. Ruling-class girls learned a similar sense of duty, but were generally treated very differently from their brothers. Girls were often educated at home by **governesses**, and were brought up to be young ladies, skilled mainly in domestic arts like cooking and

> 'Of all the European peoples we are the one that cares least about children ... We are selfish and like our enjoyments, and we find that pets give us less trouble.'
>
> Gerald Brenan, British writer and the author of *The Spanish Labyrinth*

sewing; any serious intellectual interest was actively discouraged. Their future was to be the wives and mothers of the governing elite.

If the treatment of upper-class children seems cruel to the modern observer, it is nothing compared with the treatment of poor children. In the late 18th and early 19th centuries, during the first phase of the industrial revolution, many thousands of children, some as young as five or six years old, were employed for more than twelve hours a day, six days a week, in dirty, dangerous and extremely tiring work. Some worked as chimney sweeps and many more in factories, where they were expected to work and maintain dangerous machinery, or down coal mines, where they opened and closed the ventilation doors.

Such exploitation has rightly become notorious. Yet it should not be forgotten that the Victorians introduced wide-ranging laws governing the treatment of children. In 1842, the Coal Mines Act banned the employment underground of boys aged under ten years and all women and girls, irrespective of age. Two years later, the Factory Act introduced a 'half-time' day for children aged under thirteen years as well as three hours' compulsory education. Six million new school places were provided in 1870 and elementary education became free and compulsory to the age of ten. By the start of the 20th century, the minimum age of employment had been raised to 12 and a maximum working week of 30 hours enforced.

During the 20th century, attitudes to children among the working class changed. The Second World War had involved the traumatic evacuation of well over one million children from the cities to the countryside, the separation of families and the loss of young lives in bombing raids. In the post-war era, this seems to have highlighted the importance of children and the need to provide them with loving care. It also became easier to limit family size, which meant that children could be enjoyed. This was reinforced by the better living standards and job security in the years after 1945. In recent decades, however, there have been growing concerns that this process has gone too far. Children are said to have become pampered and indulged, and over-cautious parents have prevented their **offspring** from discovering the independence and sense of adventure that previous generations took for granted.

There is also a darker perspective on children in modern British history. While child-abusers have always been treated with particular disgust, children themselves and their potentially brutal capacities have also been the object of suspicion and dread. *Tom Brown's Schooldays*, for example, featured terrifying examples of bullying at Rugby. The poet Philip Larkin wrote of 'children / With their shallow violent eyes.' The torture and murder of a toddler, James Bulger, by two ten-year-olds in 1993 profoundly shocked the nation and seemed to confirm people's darkest fears. In 2001, legislation allowed the police and local authorities to impose **curfews** on children aged between 10 and 15, and the government of Tony Blair also reduced the age of criminal responsibility to 10. Some argued that this represented a return to the view of children as 'miniature adults'. It certainly suggests that British attitudes to children remain deeply conflicted.

1895 advert

Glossary

boarding school	a school where children live, sleep and eat
prefects	senior pupils with particular responsibilities
sermons	religious or moral talks
governesses	private live-in female teachers
offspring	a person's child or children
curfews	bans requiring people to remain indoors between particular hours

C Check your facts!

1 'The word *child* entered the English language in 1600.' True or false?

2 Wealthy 17th-century parents did **not** seek to _______ their children.
a) educate
b) nurture
c) improve
d) exploit

3 Identify the children's author.
a) Thomas Hughes
b) Tom Brown
c) Harry Potter
d) Dr Thomas Arnold

4 'The Victorian middle classes sent their boys away to boarding schools to help make them tough leaders of the future.' True or false?

5 Dr Thomas Arnold was headmaster of:
a) Eton.
b) Rugby.
c) Harrow.
d) Marlborough.

6 How many hours a week might a five-year-old work in the early 19th century?

7 'The 1842 Coal Mines Act meant that only people over ten years old could work underground.' True or false?

8 What happened during the Second World War to change attitudes towards children?
a) limiting family size got easier
b) living standards improved
c) job security increased
d) families became separated

9 What two changes in the law regarding children did the Blair government make?

D What do you think?

1 Explain in your own words what you think the difference is between a child and a 'miniature adult'.

2 What does English children's literature have in common with the reality of childhood as depicted in this text?

3 Who would definitely not be surprised to learn that Britain had a society to protect animals before it had one to protect children?
a) Gerald Brenan
b) Enid Blyton
c) Dr Thomas Arnold
d) Philip Larkin

4 'The author of this text condemns the Victorian attitude to children in all its aspects.' True or false? Give reasons.

5 What evidence is there in the text to suggest that in modern times the British have not become softer on their children?

Thomas Arnold

Section 2: *Topic development*

A 'Kids' – dictionary skills

In English we use many different words for *child*, depending on factors such as the age of the child in question, the level of formality required and the attitude we want to express.

1 Working with a partner, fill in as many details as you can about the words below that you know.

2 Then use a dictionary to complete the table as best you can. Some of the boxes can stay empty. A few details have already been filled in for you as an example.

Word	Age?	Formality?	Attitude expressed?
child		*neutral*	
youngster			
little one			*affection*
baby			
babe-in-arms			
infant			
tot	*0-1 year*		
toddler			
newborn			
lad		*informal*	
lass			
kid			
kiddywink			
teen, teenager	*13-19 years*		
juvenile		*formal*	
youth			
adolescent			
brat			*dislike*
minor			

3 Now discuss in groups which of these words you would use to describe any children you know. How much would it depend on the situation?

4 How many words does your language have for children?

B Dickens on child labour

The great Victorian writer, Charles Dickens, used his novels to criticize the new industrial society developing around him. In *David Copperfield*, which tells the story of a 'self-made man', he drew on his own experiences as a 12-year-old child labourer to convey the misery it involved:

It is a matter of some surprise to me, even now, that I can have been so easily thrown away at such an age. A child of excellent abilities and with strong powers of observation, quick, eager, delicate, and soon hurt bodily or mentally, it seems wonderful to me that nobody should have made any [effort to save me]. But none was made; and I became, at ten years old, a little [labourer] in the service of Murdstone & Grinby.

Later David Copperfield describes how he felt about the rough boys he worked with:

No words can express the secret agony of my soul as I sunk into this companionship ... and felt my hopes of growing up [illegible]tinguished man crushed in my bosom.

1 What was the worst thing [illegible] David Copperfield/Charles Dickens?
2 Describe the personality of [illegible] Copperfield.
3 What does *wonderful* mean in common usage today?
4 Read the first passage carefully and say if you think it meant the same thing in Dickens' day?
5 What does this teach us about language?

C Childish or childlike?

These two words have a very similar meaning, but their **connotations** – the special sense in which people understand them – are different.

Discuss with a partner what you think the difference is, thinking about which is more positive than the other.

Section 3: *Extension activities*

A Discuss

Is it better to be soft or hard with children – or a combination of both? Discuss:

- how you were brought up.
- how you are/will be with the children in your life.
- what the general culture is in your country with regard to children.
- how you think modern British parents are with their children.

B Research

Search for: 'NSPCC' / 'Enid Blyton' / 'Harry Potter' + 'books' + 'films'

1 Find out about the NSPCC.
- Who set it up and why?
- How big is it today?
- What does it do?
- How does it advertise? (see YouTube)

2 Many of our ideas about British childhood come from children's literature. Find out about Enid Blyton.
- Where was she born?
- What are her most famous books/creations?
- How many books did she write?
- Is her work still popular?

3 Find out about Harry Potter.
- Who writes the stories? Where and why did she start?
- How many Harry Potter books have sold worldwide?
- Are the Harry Potter films as popular?
- How rich is the author now?

C Write

Write an account of your childhood, covering points such as:
- where you spent it.
- who brought you up.
- brothers, sisters, cousins.
- early friendships.
- discipline and punishment.
- education.
- happy memories.
- not-so-happy memories.
- how it has influenced your adult life.

(250 words)

19 AULD ENEMIES: ENGLAND AND SCOTLAND

Section 1: *Reading*

A Before you read – think and discuss

England and Scotland were ancient national enemies who joined together to form a larger country. It has not always been a happy union.

- Who are your country's oldest enemies?
- Are they still your country's enemies?
- Can countries who have been enemies ever work well together?
- What, if anything, do you know about Scotland?

B Read the text

AULD ENEMIES: ENGLAND AND SCOTLAND

'... for as long as but a hundred of us remain alive, never will we on any conditions be brought under English rule.' ***Declaration of Arbroath, 1320***

The unofficial Scottish anthem, 'Flower of Scotland', written in 1967 and played at all major sporting events involving the national team, **commemorates** a victory over the English in 1314. The English like to joke that this was the last time Scotland won anything against them. But, in fact, like the Romans before them, the English never managed to conquer their northern neighbours.

The history between these neighbouring countries is a story of intense rivalry and conflict. In the centuries after the Romans left Britain, the English and the Scots fought many ferocious battles. Two were particularly significant. In June 1314, the 7,000 soldiers of the Scottish King Robert the Bruce humiliated the 15,000-strong army of the English King Edward II at the Battle of Bannockburn. This was the greatest military defeat suffered by the English throughout the Middle Ages. Bannockburn also enabled Robert to create a powerful independent identity for Scotland. The second battle did not have such a positive outcome for the Scots. In September 1513, the supremely self-confident King James IV of Scotland (a member of the Stuart family) declared war on England at a time when the young King Henry VIII was pursuing military glory in France. At the Battle of Flodden, the Scots suffered the heaviest defeat of their entire history after four hours of desperate hand-to-hand combat. The turning point came when James himself was cut down in the thick of the battle. The vast majority of the Scottish nobility died with him that day.

This was a devastating time in Scotland's history. However, a Stuart descendant of King James IV would eventually inherit the throne of England. In 1603, his great-grandson King James VI of Scotland also became King James I of England. This meant that for the first time there was a union of the English and Scottish crowns, though the countries retained separate parliaments. Just over a century later, however, after much pressure had been applied and financial bribes offered, a genuine political union was eventually sealed between the two countries. The Scottish Parliament voted itself out of existence and the 1707 Act of Union created the United Kingdom of Great Britain.

The monarchs of this new kingdom were not Scots but Germans – the Protestant Hanoverians. Many Scots did not believe the union was 'Great'. In the years after 1707 they actively supported the Jacobite movement, which aimed to restore the Stuarts to the throne. The Jacobites led a series of rebellions, most dramatically in 1715 and 1745. The leader of the second rebellion, known as the '45, was Prince Charles Edward Stuart – best known to history as the Young Pretender or Bonnie Prince Charlie. His troops were mainly made up of men from the Highland clans who supported the Jacobite cause. Prince Charles was spirited and daring, but his troops suffered a heavy military defeat by the Duke of Cumberland's English army at the Battle of Culloden in April 1746. The English took terrible revenge on the Scots in the wake of Culloden, hunting the rebel Highlanders down and killing them. They destroyed whole villages, rounded up people and either shot them or put them on ships to be **transported**. They banned Highland dress and Highland customs. It was, in a sense, 18th-century **ethnic cleansing**.

Surprisingly, the response to all these pressures on Scottish identity was an era of immense creativity and accomplishment known as the Scottish Enlightenment. In the 18th century Scotland became Europe's most literate society, with profound thinkers and writers such as Adam Smith (a moral philosopher and pioneer of political economics best known for *A Wealth of Nations*), David Hume (a philosopher best known for *A Treatise of Human Nature*), Robert Burns (a poet, lyricist and pioneer of the **Romantic movement**, best known for poems including 'A Red, Red Rose' and 'A Man's A Man for A' That'), and James Boswell (a lawyer, diarist and author, best known for his biography of Samuel Johnson), plus numerous architects, inventors and engineers. The Scottish Enlightenment produced an idea of modernity that shaped subsequent Western civilization.

Statue of Bonnie Prince Charlie

Battle of Bannockburn

The development and maintenance of the British Empire showed just how closely the English and the Scots could work together when they chose to, for the 1707 Act of Union was not just political; it was also a union of economies and of imperial ambitions. Scotland's **entrepreneurs**, engineers, doctors and soldiers happily **deployed** their skills and energies across the globe in the service of English capital and under the protection of England's navy. And by the mid-19th century, the Clydeside docks in Glasgow were producing more ships than anywhere else in the world. By 1911, Glasgow became the second city of the empire, with a population of just over one million.

Since the late 19th century, some of the fiercest Anglo-Scottish rivalry has been played out on the sporting field. The two nations contested the first-ever official football international in Glasgow in 1872. The Scots often seemed to take the fixture more seriously than the English; beating England at football was one way to prove that they were the equal of their much larger neighbour. From the 1930s onwards, it became a biennial tradition for tens of thousands of Scots fans – known as the Tartan Army because so many of them wore traditional Scots tartan – to travel south when the teams played at Wembley Stadium. They would fill the streets of London with their banners and revelry before and after the match. The fixture was finally abolished in 1989 because it was thought to be souring Anglo-Scottish relations.

The 1970s saw the rise of Scottish nationalism. This renewed nationalist spirit was reflected politically in support for the Scottish Nationalist Party, which campaigned for Scotland to be a separate country again. Most Scots thought Mrs Thatcher's Conservative government (1979–1990) was unsympathetic to Scottish interests, particularly economically. North Sea oil was a controversial point because it was drilled for off the coast of Scotland but the profits went to the British government. More and more people called for self-government. At the 1997 general election the Conservatives won no seats at all in Scotland. Tony Blair's triumphant Labour government carried out its promise to give the Scots a **referendum** on a Scottish Parliament. The vote was 74.3 per cent in favour of a Parliament with some tax-raising powers. A new Scottish Parliament was elected in 1999, the first for nearly 300 years. Many Britons feared this marked the beginning of the end for the union. The triumph of the pro-independence SNP in the 2011 Scottish election suggests they were right.

Glossary

commemorates	remembers with respect
transported	sent to another country as a punishment
ethnic cleansing	the killing or expelling of one ethnic group by another
Romantic movement	an 18th-century movement in the arts and literature
entrepreneurs	people who set up businesses
deployed	brought into effective action
referendum	a yes/no vote by the people on a single political question

C Check your facts!

1 'Scotland has been dominated by England since 1314.' True or false?

2 England defeated Scotland at:
a) the Battle of Bannockburn in 1513.
b) the Battle of Flodden in 1314.
c) the Battle of Bannockburn in 1314.
d) the Battle of Flodden in 1513.

3 What connected James VI of Scotland and James I of England?
a) James VI was James I's great-grandson.
b) They were one and the same person.
c) They both supported the Act of Union.
d) Neither wanted a Stuart on the English throne.

4 Write down the three full names by which the 1745 Scottish Jacobite leader was known.

5 'The loss of Scottish independence prevented the country from contributing much to European civilization.' True or false?

6 Why was Glasgow so important to the British Empire?

7 'The British government saw England–Scotland football games as a good way of promoting friendship between the two countries.' True or false?

8 Who of the following was the least sympathetic to Scottish self-government?
a) Mrs Thatcher
b) Tony Blair
c) the Scottish Nationalist Party
d) the Scottish voters

D What do you think?

1 Explain why the Act of Union in 1707 was much less popular with Scots than the Union of Crowns in 1603.

2 Having read the text, do you think Scotland has more reason to resent or to be grateful for the union with England? Explain your answer.

3 According to the text, the Scottish Enlightenment was mainly due to:
a) the rise of Scottish nationalism.
b) ethnic cleansing by the English.
c) growing literacy in Europe.
d) questions of Scottish identity.

4 'Scotland was a poor colony of England and opposed English imperialism.' True or false? Give your reasons.

5 The historic England–Scotland football match was abolished in 1989 because:
a) the Scots had ruined Wembley Stadium and made it unplayable.
b) it had a bad effect on relations between the two countries.
c) the English always won and there was no real competition.
d) the Scots took it too seriously even though it was only a game.

Section 2: *Topic development*

A Fitba boasts

'Fitba' is what Scots affectionately call their national game, football. Though in modern times English clubs and the English national team are far more successful than their Scottish equivalents, Scots take great pride in their football history. Below are some proud Scottish fitba boasts.

1 Fill in the gaps with the right word from the box.

first (x2) oldest popular most best

a) The _______ club rivalry in football is Rangers *v.* Celtic, which began in 1888.
b) The _______ people ever to attend a football match in Britain is nearly 150,000 at Hampden Park, Glasgow, in 1937.
c) The _______ British team to compete in the European Cup was the Edinburgh club Hibernian, in 1955.
d) The _______ and most _______ supporters in the world are the Tartan Army.
e) The _______ British team to win the European Cup was Glasgow Celtic, in 1967.

2 Which of the Scottish fitba boasts is a matter of **opinion** rather than a historical **fact**?

3 Discuss with a partner what sort of **evidence** you would need before you could accept this opinion as a fact.

B 'Most romantic names'

Scottish football clubs can also claim to have more romantic names than English ones. The six examples below are in alphabetical order. Work with a partner to put them in a league table of 'most romantic names'. You can check meanings in a dictionary, but your main task is to focus on the sound and associations of each name.

Write a sentence with your partner, saying why you think your league leader's name is the most romantic.

Alphabetical order	'Most romantic name' order
Hamilton Academicals	
Heart of Midlothian	
Hibernian	
Inverness Caledonian Thistle	
Motherwell	
Queen of the South	

C Invented or discovered?

1 Scotland has a long tradition of invention and discovery. Discuss with your partner the difference between **inventing** something and **discovering** it.

2 Work together to complete the chart below, joining the four columns as in the example.

The mackintosh ('mac')	was	discovered	by	Alexander Fleming.
The pneumatic tyre	were	invented		John Logie Baird.
The telephone				Charles Mackintosh.
The pedal bicycle				Alexander Graham Bell.
The television				Kirkpatrick Macmillan.
Penicillin				John Boyd Dunlop.

TIP! **Tip! Sometimes the clue is in the name of the inventor/discoverer. In other cases your general knowledge will help you or you may need to do further research. You may also need to work by eliminating options and guessing!**

Section 3: *Extension activities*

A Discuss

Scotland lost its independence in 1707. Scots then looked to their own institutions (the church, law and education), their sports teams, to language and even to national dress for a sense of national identity. Discuss:

- whether a nation can really exist if it isn't an independent country.
- the things that best express your nation's identity.
- how you think the Scots and the English differ.
- if there really is such a thing as 'national identity'.

B Research

Search for: 'Eagle of the Ninth' / 'Auld Lang Syne' / 'Sean Connery'

1 Find out about the Roman Ninth Legion, the so-called 'Eagle of the Ninth'.
- What is its connection with Scotland?
- What is believed to have happened to it?
- What books/films/TV programmes are associated with it?

Edinburgh Castle

2 Find out about *Auld Lang Syne,* probably the most famous Scottish song in the world.
- Who wrote the song and when?
- When do people usually sing it?
- What does *Auld Lang Syne* mean?
- Is it always sung to the same tune?

3 Find out about a Scottish film star, Sean Connery.
- What role was he most famous for?
- Where was he born?
- What are his politics with regard to Scotland?
- Does he live in Scotland?

4 Find out about the Union Jack.
- What is the Union Jack?
- How is Scotland represented within it?

C Write

The quote at the beginning of the chapter is from the Declaration of Arbroath, considered to be one of the earliest declarations of independence in history. Write your own personal 'Declaration of Independence' – for yourself, your family, friends, community, nation, country or any other group you belong to. Explain:
- who you are claiming independence from.
- why you want to be free from them.
- how things will be different when you are independent.
- what you are prepared to do to achieve independence. (250 words)

20 THAT CLOUD IN THE WEST: IRELAND

Section 1: *Reading*

A Before you read – think and discuss

Britain and Ireland are separated by just a short stretch of sea. However, the long history between the two countries has not always been happy.

- Has your country fought with any of its neighbours?
- What do neighbouring countries fight about?
- How can ancient conflicts be solved?
- What, if anything, do you know about Ireland and its history?

B Read the text

'THAT CLOUD IN THE WEST'

'You have a starving population, an absentee aristocracy and an alien Church … That is the Irish question.'
Benjamin Disraeli (later British prime minister) to Parliament, 1844

It has been said that Ireland suffers from having too much history and this is certainly true of its history with Britain. Direct British influence over Ireland dates back to the reign of King Henry II in the late 12th century, and since then, Anglo-Irish relations have rarely been harmonious.

The United Kingdom of Great Britain and Ireland was formed by an Act of Union on 1st January 1801 after the Irish Parliament in Dublin voted itself out of existence. Britain, always the dominant power in the relationship, feared that Ireland would become the base for a French invasion. One historian has said, 'From a British point of view the Union was little short of military necessity.'

The Union made Irish grievances against the British worse. Many of the problems stemmed from the inequality between the two sections of the population. Most of the population (85 per cent) was Catholic, but most of the land was owned by English Protestants. To make matters worse, since the 17th century, British rule had identified Roman Catholics as enemies of the constitution and denied them all political rights. When the prime minister, William Pitt the Younger, tried to reverse this situation, King George III prevented him. He claimed this would be to go against the oath he had sworn on becoming king in 1760, as 'defender of the faith' – the *Protestant* faith.

Although Catholics were eventually granted political rights in 1829, Ireland's fragile economy had reached breaking point. A major problem was the staggeringly rapid growth of the population. By 1845, this had passed 8 million, or over one-third of the population of the United Kingdom. Such growth proved unsustainable when a fungal disease destroyed half the Irish potato crop in 1845. A near-total crop failure followed in 1846 and again in 1848. As Ireland's population was largely dependent on the potato for food, over one million people died of starvation and disease. An even greater number were forced to emigrate – to Canada, Australia, New Zealand, the United States and Great Britain. To this day, most people believe that the British government could and should have done far more to help the starving Irish. Ireland was the only country in Europe to have a lower population in 1900 than it had in 1800.

The late 19th century saw growing unrest in Ireland, with Charles Stewart Parnell leading calls for Home Rule. Anglo-Irish relations were dominated by the actions of the Liberal politician W. E. Gladstone. After the general election of 1868, Gladstone was the leader of the largest political party in Parliament. He received his formal summons from Queen Victoria to form a new government while chopping down trees on his family estate. He carefully put down his axe and told the **bemused** messenger: 'My mission is to pacify Ireland.'

Gladstone

Michael Collins, IRA

Gladstone's mission was a failure, but arguably a heroic one. Gladstone was head of four separate governments between 1868 and 1894 and introduced various laws dealing with the Irish church, the land, the legal system and voting rights. There were those who thought that the Irish question obsessed him. His goal was not independence for Ireland but political freedoms *within* the UK similar to those enjoyed by Scotland today. To this end, in 1886 and 1893 Gladstone introduced Home Rule Bills that aroused feverish debate. On one occasion, there was even a fight in Parliament involving some 80 MPs. Ultimately, though, both bills were rejected and the British Liberal Party came close to collapse.

Gladstone suffered savage personal criticism over Home Rule for Ireland. Lord Randolph Churchill (Winston Churchill's father) called him 'an old man in a hurry'. One Conservative MP said he was **'half-cracked'**.

Despite the criticism, Gladstone's party thought that it had cracked the Irish question in 1914. The Liberal government of H. H. Asquith managed to pass a Home Rule Bill almost identical to Gladstone's. But in carrying through this reform, Asquith faced a significant new enemy – armed Loyalists from **Ulster**. These Ulster Unionists threatened civil war in Ireland if Home Rule (they called it 'Rome Rule') was forced on them. Civil war was averted by the outbreak of the First World War, with the Home Rule Act being suspended for its duration. By 1918, however, Irish politics had been transformed by the rise of Republicanism. The Republican political party Sinn Féin ('we ourselves') demanded complete independence from the United Kingdom. Home Rule was now dead and violence followed.

Since 1922, there have been two Irelands. Northern Ireland has remained part of the UK, while the rest of the country has been independent. But Catholic Republicans in Northern Ireland, opposed to any part of Ireland remaining under British rule, ultimately rose up against the dominant Protestant majority. Between the late 1960s and late 1990s, Northern Ireland was scarred by violent civil conflict known as the Troubles. Over 3,700 people lost their lives as a result of terrorist bombings and shootings by the Catholic IRA, Protestant UDA and other **paramilitary** organizations. Many innocent people also died as the result of actions by the British army and Ulster police. In the early period of Tony Blair's premiership, the Good Friday Agreement (1998) was signed, effectively ending hostilities. There was widespread celebration and Blair said he felt 'the hand of history' on his shoulder. Perhaps there was an answer to the Irish question after all.

Glossary

bemused	puzzled, confused
half-cracked	half-mad
Ulster	the nine most Protestant counties of Ireland (situated in the north-east)
paramilitary	organized like an army

C Check your facts!

1 'Britain has been directly involved in Irish affairs for over a thousand years.' True or false?

2 Britain wanted a union with Ireland in 1801 mainly because it feared:
a) a French invasion from Ireland.
b) an Irish invasion from France.
c) an Irish–French invasion.
d) all of the above.

3 Why did George III refuse to give Irish Catholics political rights?

4 How much of the Irish potato crop was destroyed by disease in 1845?
a) 30 per cent
b) 50 per cent
c) most of it
d) all of it

5 Why did Queen Victoria call on Gladstone to form a government in 1868?

6 'Gladstone's mission was to give Ireland its independence.' True or false?

7 'Gladstone tried so hard with Ireland only because it made him popular.' True or false?

8 What stopped the Irish getting Home Rule in 1914?

9 How long did the Troubles last?

D What do you think?

1 Was 'the United Kingdom of Great Britain and Ireland' truly a united kingdom? Explain your answer.

2 The British could **not** fairly be blamed for:
a) the fungal disease in potatoes.
b) poverty and starvation in Ireland.
c) mass Irish emigration.
d) injustice suffered by Catholics.

3 Gladstone was probably chopping down trees because:
a) he was an old man in a hurry.
b) he was half-cracked.
c) he was trying to pacify Ireland.
d) he found the exercise beneficial.

4 '... the Irish question had finally been cracked' means that it had been:
a) solved or answered.
b) divided into two parts.
c) judged to be mad.
d) asked in the right way.

5 During the Troubles, the two groups who wanted British rule in Northern Ireland to continue were:
a) the British and Irish governments.
b) Republicans and Loyalists.
c) the British Army and paramilitary groups.
d) Loyalists and the British government.

Section 2: *Topic development*

A The famine

1 Look at this photo. What do you think the sculpture shows?

2 This memorial to the famine stands in Dublin, capital of the Republic of Ireland.

   a) Who do you think each of the figures is? How do the figures relate to each other?
   b) Is this memorial different from traditional statues and civic monuments?
   c) How does it make you feel?
   d) How do you think it makes ordinary Dubliners feel as they go about their lives?
   e) Can you think of any other memorials like this?
   f) Do you think this kind of memorial is a good or bad idea?

B What could have been done to help the Irish?

To this day, most people believe that the British government could and should have done far more to help the starving Irish.

1 Read the text below, which develops the point made in the extract above, and discuss the difference in meaning between *could have*, *should have*, *might have* and *needed to*.

Many Irish historians have argued that the British government

could have taken steps to ensure that imported food was distributed to those Irish in greatest need.
should have been willing to treat the famine crisis in Ireland as an imperial responsibility and to pay for relief.
might have prohibited the export of grain from Ireland.

Historians also add two other ideas:

The amount of money that the government spent on public works in Ireland **needed to be** much higher.
The poor-law system of providing relief for the starving Irish **needed to be** much less restrictive.

2 Think about one of the biggest disappointments in your life. Write about what happened and how you feel about it now. Then write sentences about what a) *would have happened*, b) *should have happened*, c) *could have happened* and d) *might have happened* instead.

C The political weather

1 Label pictures 1–6 with words from the box.

rainbow   shower   sunlit uplands   weather vane   wind   storm

1

____

2

____

3

____

4

____

5

____

6

____

2 The title for this chapter is taken from a phrase in a famous speech by Gladstone: 'Ireland, Ireland! That cloud in the west! That coming storm!' In English, there is a long tradition of describing politics in terms of the weather. Read the quotes below and study the idioms in bold. What do you think they mean? Discuss your ideas.

a) Between 1994 and 1997, Fine Gael, the Labour Party and the Democratic Left, the three main parties of the Irish republic, governed in the so-called **'Rainbow Coalition'**.

b) They have spent millions without reaching any answers – what **a shower** of wasters!

c) [Tony Blair] has no rooted ideology whatsoever and is **a political weathervane** subject to any **puff of hot air**.

d) Smith has always shown an ability to sense which way **the political wind** is blowing and has changed his mind accordingly.

e) For all its sudden emergence recently onto what look like **sunlit uplands**, Ireland has had a history of hardship, and one can't blame them for not wanting to go back there.

f) Eventually he was recalled to England where he died as the great **political storm** in Ireland brewed.

3 Now write a political weather forecast for your country for the next two/three years. Use at least **three** of the idioms.

The political weather in my country over the next two/three years will be/is going to be ...
(Remember that *going to* implies a stronger prediction, based on evidence, than *will*.)

Section 3: *Extension activities*

A Discuss

Gladstone believed that his mission was to pacify Ireland, but many believe all his efforts amounted to nothing more than a heroic failure. Discuss:

- if failure can really be considered heroic.
- whether it is a good thing for politicians to have a sense of mission.
- what new missions the world might need (e.g., to save the economy, environment).

B Research

Search for: 'Saint Patrick' / 'Fields of Athenry' + 'Glasgow Celtic FC' + 'Liverpool FC' / 'Irish pub' + (a city of your choice)

1 Find out about the patron saint of Ireland, St Patrick.
- Where was he born?
- On which date is he celebrated?
- How do people all over the world mark his day?
- What do they drink?

2 Search for the song 'The Fields of Athenry' and read the lyrics.
- Who wrote the song and when?
- What story does it tell?
- Why do fans of the Scottish football team Glasgow Celtic sing it?

3 Search on the Internet to find a city in the world that does not have an Irish pub.
- Can you find one?
- Discuss why there are so many Irish pubs all over the world.
- What does it tell you about a) the Irish and b) how people feel about the Irish?

C Write

1 Write about your country's history and one of its big 'questions' (problems). Include:
- what the question is.
- when it started.
- why it started.
- what has been done about it.
- what you think the answer to it is/was. (250 words)

2 Watch a film about Irish history, such as *Fifty Dead Men Walking* (2008), *Hunger* (2008), *The Wind that Shakes the Barley* (2006) or *Michael Collins* (1996). Then write a review. Include:
- who and what the film is about.
- what happens.
- who plays the main character(s).
- your personal response to the film.
- whether you think this is a good way to learn about history. (250 words)

21 A safe haven? Immigration to Britain

Section 1: *Reading*

A Before you read – think and discuss

A long history of immigration from all over the globe has made Britain one of the most multicultural countries in the world.

- What do you know about the history of immigration to your country?
- What do you think it is like to be an immigrant to your country?
- What do you think it is like to be an immigrant to Britain?
- What, if anything, do you know about the different immigrant groups who have come to make their home in Britain?

B Read the text

A safe haven? Immigration to Britain

'It never misses ... anyone. It loves nobody, it needs nobody; it tolerates all the types of mankind.'

Ford Madox Ford (English novelist, poet and author of* The Good Soldier, *writing about London)

Extreme nationalist parties have never had much success in British politics. One possible reason for this is that Britain has always been a mixture of nations and nationalities. Even the Union Jack is a combination of the flags of the patron saints of England, Scotland and Ireland. The original inhabitants were mainly Celtic tribes, but over the centuries many immigrant groups have come to shape Britain's development.

Britain's first invaders were the Romans, who arrived in 55 BC. In the 'Dark Ages' that followed their departure in AD 410, Germanic tribes then Vikings attacked the country, settling in the south and north respectively. The last great invading force was William the Conqueror's Normans in 1066, but **paradoxically** once invasion ended, immigration began.

One of William's first acts was to invite Jewish merchants from France to England in the belief that they would help make the country richer. Christian–Jewish relations were good for a time, but increasing Christian intolerance led to **persecution**, massacres and the expulsion of all Jews in 1290. It was not until 1655 that Oliver Cromwell lifted the ban on them. Like William, he believed they could help the economy. Growing tolerance in the 18th and 19th centuries was sealed by formal Jewish emancipation in 1858, which allowed Jews to sit in Parliament.

The biggest-ever wave of Jewish immigration to Britain came in the 1880s and 1890s, triggered by massacres in the Russian Empire. By 1919 there were about 250,000 Jews in Britain. The Aliens Act of 1905 restricted the flood of immigration, and there was some anti-semitism in the 1930s, but there was never actual persecution. In London's Cable Street in October 1936, local people rose up to repel a fascist march through the Jewish East End, and for a time Britain was a **refuge** for Jews escaping Nazi Germany. But in 1938 the Government banned all further immigration, making an exception for 10,000 Jewish children who came from Nazi-occupied Europe on a rescue mission known as the *Kindertransport*. They also **interned** German Jews at the start of the Second World War. Despite these restrictions, however, most British Jews consider their country to have been a model of tolerance compared with its European neighbours.

Britain's tradition of religious tolerance can also be seen in the case of the Huguenots. About 50,000 of these French Protestants **sought asylum** in Britain after Louis XIV made their religion illegal in 1685. The 18th-century French thinker, Voltaire, was so impressed by British liberty that he asked: 'Why can't the world be more like England?'

While some came to Britain for freedom, others came for money. By far the biggest group of economic migrants in British history is the Irish. About 10 per cent of British people today have at least one Irish grandparent, and there are significant Irish communities in most urban centres. Irish workers – known as 'navvies' – helped to build Britain's canal network in the late 18th century and then the railways from the 1830s onwards. Though conditions on the railways were terrible, the Great Famine in Ireland of the 1840s ensured a steady supply of Irish labour came to Britain. The difficult economic conditions of mid-20th-century Ireland had the same effect, with Irish workers predominating in construction and road-building. Despite their huge contribution, many British natives treated Irish immigrants with contempt and prejudice. This often gave way to deep suspicion and hostility during the IRA terrorist bombing campaigns from the 1970s to the early 1990s. But on the whole, the story of the Irish in Britain has been one of integration and acceptance.

Membership of the British Empire, and the Commonwealth which replaced it, offered many other groups the chance to come to Britain as economic migrants. The British Nationality Act of 1948 – passed to help with Britain's labour shortage after the Second World War – gave 800 million people the right to live and work in the UK without a visa. Of the many hundreds of thousands who came, the largest group was from the Indian subcontinent, who mostly found jobs in public transport and textiles.

The second largest group of immigrants came from the Caribbean. They became known as the 'Windrush generation',

Enoch Powell

after the *Empire Windrush* ship which arrived in June 1948 with 492 Jamaican immigrants on board. They found jobs in public transport and did the sort of **menial** work which many did not want to do. These new arrivals often met with racism and hostility, and restrictions on Commonwealth immigration came in the late 1960s and early 1970s. The fears of many others were vividly expressed by the right-wing politician Enoch Powell in his notorious 'Rivers of Blood' speech of April 1968, which predicted that the racial mixing of Britain would lead to bloodshed. In 1981, serious rioting broke out in Brixton, a predominantly black area of London, and some concluded that Powell had been proved right. But in fact, Brixton has been largely peaceful since then and race relations in Britain have improved. Mixed-race people became the fastest-growing ethnic group. And though the 1972 Immigration Act put a stop to mass immigration from the Commonwealth, the Government made an exception in the case of 27,000 Ugandan Asians suffering persecution by Idi Amin.

The collapse of the Soviet Union in 1991 and the expansion of the EU led to a wave of Eastern European immigration, above all from Poland. Britain was one of the few countries to open its doors immediately to citizens of new EU member states. By 2008, over one million had come, finding work in service industries, construction and other skilled trades. So while the British have a reputation for being cold and reserved, the facts tell another story: of one of the most open and diverse societies in human history, enriched over the centuries by successive waves of immigration.

Glossary

paradoxically	in a way that is true though it seems absurd
persecution	abuse and victimisation
refuge	a safe place
interned	put in prison for political reasons
sought asylum	came for state protection
menial	unskilled, low status

C Check your facts!

1 The Union Jack reflects Britain's:
a) extreme nationalism.
b) Celtic past.
c) immigrant history.
d) mixed character.

2 'Britain's first immigrants were Romans.' True or false?

3 Which of these dates in British history would British Jews **not** have a reason to celebrate?
a) 1066
b) 1290
c) 1655
d) 1858

4 'The biggest wave of Jewish immigration to Britain was caused by the Nazis.' True or false?

5 Why did Voltaire wish the world was more like England?

6 The Irish in Britain did **not** play an important role in building:
a) the navy.
b) the canals.
c) the railways.
d) the roads.

7 What gave so many people the right to come to Britain after the Second World War?

8 'Immigrants from the Caribbean were always warmly welcomed in Britain.' True or false?

9 Which of these was **not** a factor in bringing so many Poles to Britain in recent times?
a) the collapse of the Soviet Union
b) the expansion of the EU
c) Britain's open-door policy
d) traditional British reserve

D What do you think?

1 Of the immigrant groups mentioned, which was a) the first, b) the largest, and c) the most recent to arrive?

2 Explain in your own words the difference between an invader and an immigrant.

3 Give at least three reasons for people immigrating to Britain over the course of its history.

4 Find two facts in the text that strongly suggest Enoch Powell was wrong.

5 Say which groups came to Britain as a) asylum seekers and b) economic migrants. Did any of the groups come as both of these?

Voltaire

Section 2: *Topic development*

A Pukka chuddies: immigrant words

Just as Britain is a mixture of nations, so English contains words mixed in from other languages, including those of its immigrants. Here is a sample of just ten such words (there are many thousands of others!).

chuddies	*chutzpah*	*kushti/cushty*	*craic/crack*	*pukka*
pundit	*bling-bling*	*schlep/shlep*	*to kowtow*	*wok*

1 Do you know what any of these words mean? Discuss with a partner.

2 Now match the ten words to the following definitions. Use a dictionary if you really have no idea.

a) a bowl-shaped frying pan
b) underpants
c) show-off shiny jewellery and clothes
d) (to go on) a long boring journey
e) to do whatever others say, obey like a servant
f) proper, correct, cool
g) expert
h) lively social time, with fun conversation and laughter
i) nice and comfortable, a good situation, OK; lucky, good
j) extreme self-confidence, cheek, daring

3 Now try and match the words to their language of origin in the table below. Discuss how you think the word sounds and use that to help you guess.

Language	**Word(s)**
Hindi	
Chinese	
Irish	
Yiddish (language of East European Jews)	
Jamaican patois	
Romany (language of gypsies)	

4 Discuss in groups which of these words you like best and why.

5 Now write three sentences illustrating your three favourite words. Read them to a partner without saying the word and see if they can guess which it is.

B A poetic voyage

Read this poem about a voyage to Britain from overseas and say which immigrant group it is about. (Hint: pay special attention to the third stanza and check back in the reading passage if necessary.)

Then put the words in the box in the right place, using the context to guide you, and answer the questions that follow.

band	*Mother*	*hopefuls*	*passports*	*cold*	*blue*
British	*beginning*	*grey*	*children*	*lifetime*	*home*

It was an invitation.
An invitation to come
'Help re-build the ________ country'
It seemed like an opportunity
Jobs for everyone
A better future for our ________
Then home again
Just a few years

We left the ________ skies
The sun, the sea, the light
And then the shock
The ________ and damp
The ________ skies
The cold stares
The cold grey stares

The ship arrived on June 22nd 1948
No ________ played a welcome
492 ________ stepped ashore
Hopefuls
With our British ________ in our hands
We thought the journey had ended
It was just ________

We came for a few years
We stayed a ________ and more
Hopefuls with our British passports in our hands
They didn't think we were ________
And now our children know no other
This is their ________
And ours

1 A lot of this poem's power comes from its **contrasts**. Make a list of these, starting with the different skies of home and of Britain.

2 What does the poem say about the attitude of the British people to these new immigrants, if anything?

3 Do you think this poem was written by a man or woman, young or old person, black or white person? Give reasons.

4 Do you think the poem gives a more positive or negative view of immigration to Britain? Say why.

5 Write down in your own words how the poem makes you feel.

6 Now discuss your answers in small groups.

Section 3: *Extension activities*

A Discuss

Mohammed (and its variants) is now one of the most common names given to baby boys born in Britain. Discuss:

- what you think this tells us about modern Britain.
- how important names are culturally.
- whether you think it is better for immigrants to Britain to give their babies a) names that reflect their own culture or b) traditional British names (the law says they can do either).
- what immigrants to your country should call their children. Are there any rules about this?

B Research

Search for: 'fish and chips' / 'Brick Lane' / 'Goodness Gracious Me' + 'going out for an English'

1 Find out about fish and chips.

- What is the traditional importance of this dish in British life?
- When was it invented?
- Which immigrant groups is it associated with?
- What regional/national variations are there in how it is prepared and served?

2 Find out about Brick Lane.

- Where is it?
- Which immigrant community is it associated with today?
- Which other immigrant communities is it associated with historically?
- How does the Great London Mosque/London Jamme Masjid reflect this?
- Who wrote the prize-winning novel *Brick Lane*, and when was it made into a film?

3 Find out about the TV series *Goodness Gracious Me* and its famous 'going out for an English' sketch (available on *YouTube*).

- What was this TV series all about?
- Where did the title come from?
- What is the joke in the 'going out for an English' sketch?
- What do you think *Goodness Gracious Me* tells us about the Indian community's relationship with Britain?

C Write

Is Britain a good country for immigrants? Give your honest opinion, writing about aspects such as:

- people's attitudes.
- culture and social life.
- the economy.
- politics.
- education.
- the weather and environment. (250 words)

22 AN ENDURING OBSESSION: SOCIAL CLASS IN BRITAIN

Section 1: *Reading*

A Before you read – think and discuss

Most British politicians say they favour a fair and open society. Britain remains, however, a country of deep class divisions.

- Is your country divided along class lines?
- Is social class important?
- What, if anything, do you know about the British class system?

B Read the text

AN ENDURING OBSESSION – CLASS

'THAT TOPIC ALL-ABSORBING ... IS NOW AND EVER SHALL BE, TO US – CLASS.'

John Betjeman – English poet, writer and broadcaster

FACT FILE

- 1066: Norman invasion establishes a new aristocracy
- 19th-century village structure – freeholders, copyholders, cottagers, farm servants
- 1894: death duty introduced – leads to break-up of many large estates
- Parliament Act 1911 – prohibits the House of Lords from blocking legislation
- 1922: Andrew Bonar Law becomes the first member of the professional classes to become Prime Minister
- 1926: General Strike
- 1927: BBC established and sets the tone for the British middle classes

HISTORY OF THE CLASS SYSTEM

The British have often seemed obsessed with social class. Supporters of the class system have traditionally accepted it as a natural and unifying force. They support the idea that people should admire and respect their 'betters'. Others view it as a social evil, the root of most problems in British history.

Much of the class system dates back to 1066, when William the Conqueror, Duke of Normandy in France, invaded England. He defeated the Saxon king, Harold, at the Battle of Hastings. The Norman invasion established a new aristocracy and from that time, the English found countless ways to distinguish the descendants of Norman nobility from those of Saxon peasants. Class divisions were therefore cultural as well as economic.

The main role of the aristocracy was to support the monarchy. The nobility – historically the largest landowners – gained their titles from the monarch. They were divided into five **ranks**: dukes, marquises, earls, viscounts and barons. All were hereditary, passing down the family line. Beyond the ceremony and splendid displays, those with titles also had real political power, usually as members of the House of Lords. So the upper class was also Britain's ruling class.

The class system worked at all levels of society, not just among the elite. In pre-19th-century agricultural Britain, status was based on birth, not merit. Sons followed in the footsteps of fathers. People did not ask a boy what he was going to be when he grew up: they knew because jobs were inherited rather than chosen. The family hierarchy was rigid: the father at the head, the eldest son ranking before the younger and sons before daughters. The village structure mirrored this. The lord of the manor was the **patriarch**, and below him were different grades of people working the land. Freeholders ranked above copyholders, copyholders above cottagers, cottagers above farm servants. A verse from a 19th-century hymn reflected the permanence of this state of affairs:

The rich man in his castle
The poor man at his gate
God made them high and lowly
And ordered their estate.

THE RISE OF THE WORKING CLASS

Then the industrial revolution created the working class, and with it new class tensions. The capitalist system now dominated, with workers earning (low) wages for mainly unskilled work in the new machine-based industries and bosses profiting from their labour. People began to think differently about how power was used in society. Working-class consciousness grew. In the 1830s and 1840s, there was intense trade union conflict associated with political and economic change. Further periods of intense industrial conflict occurred in the 1880s and in the first quarter of the 20th century, culminating in the General Strike.

CLASS STRUCTURE IN THE 20TH CENTURY

By the early 20th century, people generally (and crudely) saw the class structure in terms of three main groups. Certain stereotypes characterized each group: the image of the upper classes was of top hats, stately homes, land ownership and foxhunting. The middle classes were professional, suburban, wore **trilbies**, owned their homes and liked gardening and rugby. The working classes were council tenants who wore cloth caps and enjoyed going to the pub or to a football match. On average, 60 per cent of the population described themselves as working class, compared with 30 per cent middle class and 10 per cent upper class.

THE MIDDLE CLASS EMERGES

In the late 19th century, the upper class lost much of its wealth as a result of a new death duty (later known as inheritance tax). A loss of political power followed with the 1911 Parliament Act. The middle class emerged in the 20th century as the dominant class – politically, economically and culturally. In 1922, Andrew Bonar Law became the first British prime minister from a business background. Meanwhile, the number of professional people and people earning salaries increased rapidly, especially in the state sector and in large corporations.

THE ROLE OF THE BBC

Arguably, nothing in the 20th century reflects the profound cultural influence of the middle class quite like the British Broadcasting Corporation (BBC), which quickly gained worldwide influence. The first director-general, John Reith, set its tone. He wanted the BBC to be authoritative, **impartial** and to embody the values of the educated classes. Before employing staff, managers would consider one key question: 'Is he a gentleman?' In order to convince listeners of their culture, experience and knowledge, all BBC radio announcers had to remain anonymous and wear dinner jackets when broadcasting. They also had to use Received Pronunciation (RP), a strictly formal style of speech.

A 'CLASSLESS SOCIETY'?

In recent times, a number of politicians have boasted of creating a 'classless society'. Such a society would embrace **meritocracy** and social and economic mobility – all would have an equal chance. But these claims have usually been met with contempt. The nature of the classes may have changed, but the barriers between them are the same: money, education, family and occupation. However, Britain has never been a fertile soil for Marxism. A working-class MP once dismissed the ideology as 'the fluttering of continental magpies'. But no one who studies British history can deny that class has profoundly shaped its course.

Glossary

ranks	positions within a fixed hierarchy
patriarch	the male head of a community or congregation
trilby	soft hat with a narrow brim
impartial	treating all sides equally
meritocracy	a society based on people's skills and abilities, rather than class

C Check your facts!

1 'The British have always seen class as something that unites them.' True or false?

2 Which key class distinction started in 1066?

3 The aristocracy is **not** the same thing as:
a) the upper classes.
b) the monarchy.
c) the nobility.
d) members of the House of Lords.

4 Who was at the very bottom of the old agricultural hierarchy in Britain?
a) the youngest sons of cottagers
b) the daughters of farm servants
c) the daughters of copyholders
d) the eldest sons of farm servants

5 Which new class appeared in the 19th century?

6 According to the text, the upper classes wore:
a) bowler hats.
b) trilbies.
c) top hats.
d) cloth caps.

7 What two things damaged the upper classes' economic and political power in the late 19th and early 20th centuries?

8 Who was Sir John Reith and why was he important in terms of class?

9 Does the author suggest Britain is becoming more classless?

D What do you think?

1 Does the author suggest that class is a matter of simple economics? Explain your answer.

2 The author doesn't describe how religion has affected the class system in Britain, but suggests that its role is:
a) to challenge it.
b) to support it.
c) not important.
d) impossible to know.

3 Do you think the description of the three classes in the 20th century is a broad stereotype or an exact picture of the historical reality? Explain your answer.

4 Do you think the description of the three classes includes the women who belonged to them? Give reasons.

5 John Betjeman in the quote at the beginning of the text suggests that the 'enduring obsession' belongs to:
a) all classes.
b) just the upper classes.
c) just the middle classes.
d) just the working classes.

Section 2: *Topic development*

A Posh* or not?

*upper class

Historically, you could tell a person's social class in Britain from the words they used for everyday things.

1 Match each word below with another word of the same meaning.

> dinner glasses greens ill lavatory front room settee/couch sick sitting room sofa spectacles supper toilet vegetables

dinner = supper

2 For each pair of words, decide which word is posh and which is ordinary.

3 Discuss the following questions.

- Which of the words above do you use? Have you been using the posh word or the ordinary word?
- How do you feel about this?
- In future, will you use different words? Why?
- Does it matter which word you use? Why?
- Do you think British people still care about these differences?

B Middle-class politeness

The British middle class has traditionally had a reputation for politeness, restraint and understatement.

1 Read examples of middle-class understatement a)–i). Match them to the more direct equivalents i)–ix).

a) Would it be too much to ask for some small contribution towards the cost? __
b) Would you care to join us? __
c) We are feeling a trifle peckish. __
d) It has been rather a long day. __
e) I'd rather not, if you don't mind. __
f) Could you possibly transfer the condiments to this end of the table? __
g) That would be a bit of a blow. __
h) It was very good in parts. __
i) I was wondering if you would be so kind as to refrain from smoking. __

i) No smoking!
ii) It was absolute rubbish.
iii) Come with us.
iv) We're starving!/Where's the food?
v) I'm exhausted.
vi) Pass the salt.
vii) No way!
viii) That would be a complete disaster.
ix) Come on, pay up.

2 Discuss the following questions.

- What devices do very proper English people use to make their language polite? Think about vocabulary and grammar.
- Do people use understatement in your country, or are people generally more direct?
- Do you prefer people to be very polite or more direct? Why?
- Have British people you have met been polite like this? If you have never met a real British person, what about British people in films, books or on TV – or British people your family or friends have met?

3 Work in pairs. Think of three simple requests and write them as politely as possible. Read your polite requests to another pair. Do they understand what you are asking for? Finally, refuse the other pair's three requests as politely as you can.

C Estuary English, Mockney and rhyming slang

British people – including the royal family – are increasingly speaking in a more ordinary way. Many people in London and the south-east of England now speak **Estuary English** (an accent defined as spreading outwards from London, which contains features of both Received Pronunciation and London speech). Estuary English has become dominant, reflecting the economic importance of London and the power of the London-based media.

'**Mockney**' is the name given to the accent of middle- and upper-middle-class people who adopt the traditional Cockney accent of the London working class because they think it sounds 'cool'.

Estuary English and Mockney speakers sometimes use **Cockney rhyming slang**, a kind of secret code invented by 19th-century inhabitants of the East End of London. It is based on rhyme: *Apples and pears* rhymes with *stairs,* so *I'm going up the apples and pears* means *I'm going up the stairs. Mince pies* rhymes with *eyes*, so *use your mince pies* means *use your eyes*. Sometimes only the first part of the rhyming phrase is said: *loaf of bread* rhymes with *head*, so *use your loaf* means *use your head*.

1 Use your *loaf (!)* to work out what the examples of Cockney rhyming slang in bold mean. Words that are often dropped are in brackets.

a) Would you **Adam (and Eve)** it? They've sold our best player to the other side! believe

b) Have a **butcher's (hook)** at this – it's beautifully made, isn't it? __________

c) Of course you can trust him – just look at his honest **boat (race)**. __________

d) If I don't see you before then, we can speak on the **dog (and bone)**. __________

e) We all went out to an Indian restaurant to celebrate with a **Ruby (Murray)**. __________

f) He always dresses so smartly – just look at that **whistle (and flute)** he's wearing. __________

g) You need to go to the barber and get your **Barnet (Fair)** sorted out. __________

h) We had a nice little **bowler (hat)** on the train. In fact, I was talking so much I nearly missed my stop. __________

i) She's that girl who lives down the **frog (and toad)**. I've known her for years. __________

j) He hasn't been the same since he split up from his **trouble (and strife)**. __________

2 Which of these rhyming words do you like best? Why? Choose two that you will try to use in future when speaking English informally.

Section 3: *Extension activities*

A Discuss

What role has social class played in your life? Discuss the following questions.

- What class do you consider yourself to belong to?
- What class do your parents belong to?
- Are you happy with your class status?
- How much do you think about class status?
- Has social class held you back or helped you in life?

B Research

Search for: 'posh' + 'Class' + 'John Cleese' + 'Ronnie Corbett' + 'Ronnie Barker' / 'public schools' + 'UK'

1 Find out about the origin of the word *posh*.

- What connection with India and the British Empire do people think it has?
- Are they right?

2 Watch the classic comedy sketch *Class* on the Internet. It stars John Cleese, Ronnie Barker and Ronnie Corbett.

- Who knows his place?
- Who says he doesn't have money?
- Who is said to be vulgar?
- What hats do they each wear?

3 Find out about British public schools.

- Name three of the most famous public schools.
- About how much per year does it cost to send a child to one of these schools?
- Why are they called public schools?
- Do you think this is a good term for them? Why/why not?

C Write

Which class of people would you most or least like to have belonged to in history? Write a short essay, including the following points:

- the class of people you chose, and why
- what their lives would have been like
- if you think they deserved the lives they had
- if you think you are luckier than them

(250 words)

GLOSSARY

absolutism power without limits
absolutist believing in royal power without limits (see Chapter 5)
Admiralty government department responsible for the Navy
adultery having sex with someone other than your marriage partner
archers soldiers with bows and arrows
Armada (historical) armed Spanish fleet
assertion claim
authoritarian bossy, controlling

backlash strong negative reaction
'backstreet' abortion an illegal abortion carried out by an untrained person, often in dirty conditions
ballot vote
barbarian a person who does not belong to one of the major civilizations of Greece, Rome or Christianity and is therefore thought to be uncivilized
beacon warning/signal
bemused puzzled, confused
benign gentle and kind
Bill of Rights a written statement of the rights of the people
boarding school a school where children live, sleep and eat

capital punishment putting to death by the state
catchphrase well-known phrase or slogan
cavalry soldiers on horses
characteristically in a way that is typical
charisma charm, star quality
charter a written statement of the rights of a particular group
chief protagonists main characters
chronicled recorded, told the story
clergy churchmen
commemorates remembers with respect
compulsory forced, with no element of choice
constitutional monarchy a monarchy limited by law and custom
consumer boom time of growing wealth when people buy more
cremated when the remains, usually of a dead person's body, have been burnt to ashes
curfews bans requiring people to remain indoors between particular hours

deeply flawed having big weaknesses, imperfect
demonized described as evil
deployed brought into effective action
deter put off, discourage
detractors people who are critical of someone or something
dismantled took apart

eccentric	odd, strange
electorate, the	the voters
enfranchised	having the right to vote
entrepreneurs	people who set up businesses
ethnic cleansing	the killing or expelling of one ethnic group by another
ever-diminishing	getting smaller all the time
exploitation	using for your own benefit
franchise	the right to vote in public elections
governesses	private live-in female teachers
habitable	possible to live in
haemorrhoids	swollen veins in the bottom
half-cracked	half-mad
heralded	marked the arrival of
house arrest	imprisonment in your own home
household name	a very well-known person (or thing)
hymns	religious songs
ideology	belief system
idleness	laziness, doing nothing, avoiding work
illegitimate	child born of parents not lawfully married to each other
impartial	treating all sides equally
imperialism	policy of extending a country's power and influence through colonization
impregnable	cannot be taken
inconclusive	without a winner
indigenous	native, belonging to a region
in earnest	in a serious way
in retaliation for	in revenge for
interned	put in prison for political reasons
justification	good reason for something that exists or has been done
means-tested	based on a person's income
menial	unskilled, low status
meritocracy	a society based on people's skills and abilities, rather than class
misconduct	bad behaviour
morale	enthusiasm and confidence; feeling of well-being
mourn	be sad because something/someone no longer exists
notorious	famous for something bad
obituary	an article in a newspaper about someone who has died
offspring	a person's child or children
omens	signs
ousted	removed (from a position of power)

paradoxically	in a way that is true though it seems absurd
paramilitary	organized like an army
patriarch	the male head of a community or congregation
peerless	better than anyone or anything else
persecution	abuse and victimisation
personified	represented by a person
poppies	red flowers that often grow wild in fields
potent	strongest and hardest
prefects	senior pupils with particular responsibilities
prestigious	respected, admired
prowess	skill, ability
prudish	shocked by sexual things
Puritan	extreme Protestant, believing that the Bible is the literal word of God and that man's destiny is fixed
radical	against tradition, wanting complete political or social change
ranks	positions within a fixed hierarchy
rapport	a close or sympathetic relationship
reap	gather
reap what you sow	a saying, meaning something happens to you as a result of what you have done in the past
rebellion	an attempt to remove a leader/government by force
referendum	a yes/no vote by the people on a single political question
refuge	a safe place
Restoration England	England in the reign of Charles II, after Cromwell's death
R.I.P.	rest in peace
rivalry	competition for the same outcome
robust	strong
Romantic movement	an 18th-century movement in the arts and literature
routed	completely defeated
ruthless	hard and cruel
sacred cows	most precious beliefs, above criticism
sank without trace	disappeared downwards, leaving nothing
sermons	religious or moral talks
sewerage	drains for toilet waste
slay	kill
slums	very overcrowded and bad housing occupied by poor people
social Darwinist	the idea that people are affected by the same laws of natural selection as plants and animals
soliloquies	speeches made by a character when they are 'thinking aloud'
sonnet	14-line poem with regular rhymes
sought asylum	came for state protection
sown	planted
splendours	magnificent features
sprawling	spread out irregularly over a large area
squalor	dirt, filth (especially in living conditions)

squandered	wasted
stirring	moving
stubble	what's left in the fields after crops have been cut
subservient	serving or acting in an obedient and inferior way
succeeds	takes over from (as king)
suffrage	the right to vote in political elections
swamped	flooded
sworn an oath	spoken a promise before God
thrift	being careful with money
toffs	informal and disrespectful term for members of the upper class
transported	sent to another country as a punishment
treason	betrayal of the country
trench warfare	when soldiers fight in trenches dug opposite each other, often for long periods of time and with little progress
trilby	soft hat with a narrow brim
turbulent	rough, unsettled
tyranny	cruel and oppressive rule
Ulster	the nine most Protestant counties of Ireland (situated in the north-east)
umpire	referee
unleashed	released
unprecedented	not seen before
unsordid	clean, noble
witty	clever and funny

INDEX